Robert Southwell

Twayne's English Authors Series

Arthur Kinney, Editor

University of Massachusetts, Amherst

TEAS 516

ROBERT SOUTHWELL.

By permission of the rector, Stonyhurst College.

Robert Southwell

F. W. Brownlow

Mount Holyoke College

Twayne Publishers
An Imprint of Simon & Schuster Macmillan
New York

Prentice Hall International
London Mexico City New Delhi Singapore Sydney Toronto

Twayne's English Authors Series No. 516

Robert Southwell
F. W. Brownlow

Twayne Publishers
An Imprint of Simon & Schuster Macmillan
866 Third Avenue
New York, NY 10022

Library of Congress Cataloging-in-Publication Data

Brownlow, F. W. (Frank Walsh), 1934–
Robert Southwell / by F. W. Brownlow.
p. cm.— (Twayne's English authors series; TEAS 516)
Includes bibliographical references and index.
ISBN 0-8057-7806-3
1. Southwell, Robert, Saint, 1561?–1595—Criticism and interpretation.
2. Christian literature, English—History and criticism. I. Title. II. Series.
PR2349.S5Z59 1996
821'.3—dc20 95-4883
CIP

The paper used in this publication meets the minimum requirements of American National Standard for Information Sciences—Permanence of Paper for Printed Library Materials, ANSI Z39.48-1984. ∞™

10 9 8 7 6 5 4 3 2 1

Printed in the United States of America

Contents

Editor's Note

The powerful prose and poetry of the martyred Jesuit Robert Southwell reached as wide and varied an audience in his own time as the works of Shakespeare did. Southwell's influence on the development of religious poetry in Tudor and Stuart England—especially in the work of Donne and Herbert—was immense. In this powerful and eloquent study, F. W. Brownlow shows why this was so. In Brownlow's detailed examination of this poet who thought metaphorically and who lived his life as a work of art, and in his acute critical readings of all of Southwell's works—from his *Epistle of Comfort* to his carols of Nativity and his influential lyrics—Brownlow demonstrates that Southwell's allegiance to Catholic belief and Jesuit orders caused him to be and write as he did. Out of terror, faith, and devotion, "he chose what to others was narrowness, but to him was everything." Louis Martz found in Southwell's work the basis for the English tradition of a "poetry of meditation," but Brownlow argues that it was not meditation finally—which is prayer—but poetry—which for Southwell was a perspective on life—that is his real claim on our attention. "Southwell not only wrote about sacrifice; he wrote himself as sacrifice, and lived what he had written. . . . When Robert Southwell stood in his shirt on a cold February day waiting to be hanged, he was on the threshold of achieving his own life's masterpiece and ambition." The story Brownlow tells here, based in part on recently discovered texts and manuscripts, is, like the man and his prose works and poems, unforgettable.

Arthur F. Kinney

Preface

When Henry Tudor ended the Wars of the Roses by defeating Richard III at Bosworth Field in 1485, he united England under a strong, centralized royal authority. In doing so he realized a long-standing ambition of his medieval predecessors, and he was able to bequeath that newly united, centrally governed England to his son, Henry VIII. Henceforward, under the new regime a single, undivided loyalty to the sovereign and the state would be the test of a true English subject.

One exception remained to the supremacy of the Crown. This was the Church, immensely wealthy, interwoven with English secular society at every level, and by its very nature presenting an alternative jurisdiction to the kingdoms of this world. It was inevitable that sooner or later the Church would challenge the monarchy's autonomy, and that when it did so, the monarchy would absorb it.

Nonetheless Henry VIII's nationalization of the Church of England by the Act of Supremacy in 1534 was an act of revolutionary violence, demanding a totality of allegiance that, over the long years of subsequent history, comparatively few English people have been able to give without some reservation. In fact, for many of Henry's subjects, his uniting of church and state had an effect opposite to his intention. It created, no doubt for the first time in most people's minds, a sharply drawn line of separation between the allegiances owed to the religious and secular realms. As a cause of controversy, this divisive assertion of unity separated regions, families, and friends. As a cause of war and judicial violence, it inscribed itself with appalling literalness upon the suffering bodies of the king's subjects, especially of those who, for denying the royal supremacy in religion, suffered the grimly witty penalty for the divisive crime of treason, namely to be hanged, drawn, and quartered.

All Henry's children accepted as axiomatic their father's premise that the determination of religious and educational policy lay with the Crown.[1] As a result, during the short reigns of Edward VI and Mary I, first the Catholics, then the Protestants suffered under the Crown's forcing of conscience. Finally, under the long reign of Henry's Protestant daughter Elizabeth I, the fate of virtually permanent opposition, refusal, and persecution fell upon the Catholics, who accordingly acquired the nickname "recusants," meaning "those who refuse."[2]

Specifically, Elizabethan Catholics refused to attend the services of the national church. More generally, they refused assent to the wisdom of a range of royal policies that seemed to them to be cutting the nation off from its own and its European past, and committing it to an uncongenial future. As the reign lengthened, and refusal and persecution followed each other in apparently endless succession, hope of change diminished. The Catholics found themselves dwindled in numbers, increasingly isolated, and living virtually under a kind of internment as aliens in their own country. Yet the paradox of their situation was that right up to the Civil Wars, Catholics were a considerable proportion of the population, especially in certain areas; and there was always a large number of people who, though unwilling to accept the hardships of exclusively Catholic practice under Elizabeth's government, were sympathetic to the religion. Although professed Catholics were a minority by 1600, they were a significant minority whose views, most people thought, might well prevail—an opinion that remained a possibility until the final triumph of Protestantism following the Revolution of 1688.[3]

For students of English literature, Elizabethan recusancy with all its shades of resistance to, and accommodation with, Tudor absolutism is an essential voice in the narrative of English history. No truly inclusive understanding of the English experience can exclude the recusants. Consequently, Robert Southwell, the most important of the recusant authors, is a uniquely interesting figure, a poet and prose writer set entirely apart from his establishmentarian contemporaries by his vocation, his education, his priesthood, and his martyrdom.

As a Catholic poet, committed to a pastoral use of his literary gift, Southwell spoke within and to the besieged Catholic minority. The subjects of his poems are entirely moral and religious; among them are the mysteries of religion, the experience of sin, the need for repentance, and the love of God. In his prose he instructs his people in the rules of daily Christian living; he teaches them how to mourn properly; he encourages them to keep the faith, and he comforts them against persecution. Yet despite the uniformly religious, even professional, content of much of his work, in almost all of it one feels that Southwell is writing for a larger, more critical audience than the work's ostensible recipients. The effect of his writing nearly always transcends its sectarian cause, and there seem to be two chief reasons for this.

First, as Southwell makes quite clear in the prefatory epistles to his poems, and in the dedication of *Mary Magdalen's Funeral Tears*, one of his purposes in writing was to divert contemporary English literature, especially poetry, from profane to sacred and virtuous uses.[4] To that end, he was prepared to compete on their own terms with his contemporaries, who were therefore always present to him as a highly critical, professional jury. Southwell the writer set himself very high standards, and he wrote to an audience of writers.

The second cause of Southwell's sense of writing to a larger audience was his deep patriotism. His priestly mission was directed to the entire English people: he believed that the conversion of England was not only possible, but necessary if the country was to realize its true character.[5] At the same time, his own position as an Englishman, deprived of virtually all juridical and civil rights in his own country—even of the right to exist there—meant that for him the very act of writing was a protest against current conditions in England. Merely by directing his actions and his writings to the conscience of the English people at large, he eventually found himself writing in the name of justice and right against the suppression of English liberties under the Tudor absolutism. This tendency culminated in his magnificent pamphlet *An Humble Supplication to Her Majesty,* on behalf of the oppressed Catholics.

It is very unlikely that Southwell, a superbly disciplined Jesuit intent solely upon the conversion of England to the Church's own version of the absolute state, intended his writing to have that larger significance. Yet there can be a logic in situations that transcends personal intention, and one of the ironies of his *Supplication*'s reception after his death was that it embarrassed his fellow Jesuits almost as much as it infuriated the government.[6]

As one would expect, given the sharp religious divisions of life among the English-speaking peoples, which are still evident in Northern Ireland, Robert Southwell's reputation has been preserved mostly by his co-religionists. Equally understandably, they have valued the witness of his life and death more highly than his work as a writer. Mainstream English literary history, even at its most generous and discriminating, has not known quite what to make of Southwell.[7] Hagiographically and piously inspired writing about Southwell continues to appear, but in this century, beginning with the work of the French scholar Pierre Janelle,[8] there has been a small but significant movement towards integrating Southwell's writing with his life, and in the process giving him his due place in the history of English literature.

Robert Southwell was only 33 when he died, and he produced most of his writing in English during the six years of his active life as a missionary priest in England. Some of his prose can be dated fairly precisely, but with a few exceptions his poems are datable only within the years of his mission. Given the short period of his active writing life, and the absence of precise fact, one cannot safely argue a case for stylistic or intellectual development in Southwell's work. One can, however, demonstrate its range and its power within the bounds of its tightly prescribed religious and moral subject matter. The first chapter of this book gives an account of Southwell's life and death. Then follow two chapters on his prose. The first deals with his two earlier books, *An Epistle of Comfort* and *Mary Magdalen's Funeral Tears,* and his *Epistle of Robert Southwell unto His Father.* The second discusses *The Triumphs over Death, An Humble Supplication,* and *A Short Rule of Good Life.* Chapter 4 is devoted to the long poem *Saint Peter's Complaint,* chapter 5 to the collection of 52 short poems found in the major manuscripts. The last chapter provides an overview of Southwell's reception from his own time to ours, and attempts to place him in relation to English literary tradition.

There are difficulties involved in writing about Southwell. Much, indeed most, of the writing about him is in a hagiographical or pious tradition. This is understandable, since he is in so many ways a heroic figure, especially to his fellow Catholics. On the other hand, Southwell's religion has often had a negative effect on non-Catholic readers, and over the last decade or so a kind of Protestant *revanchisme* in response to Anglo-Catholic influence on seventeenth-century studies has left almost no place in the canon for Southwell at all. Yet, as students of the period are beginning to understand, in Elizabethan England the line between Catholic and Protestant was not always clearly drawn, nor was it always drawn in the same places. In religious matters, a Catholic would find more agreement with a non-Calvinist Church of England priest like Lancelot Andrewes than with the average Protestant; but in political matters, a Catholic might well have more in common with a Protestant separatist than with an Anglican churchman. In matters of taste and culture, there may often have been no division at all. The Protestant Drayton imitated Southwell; the Catholics Southwell and Lodge were as ready to read and imitate Seneca's stoicism as any of their Protestant contemporaries.[9]

Nonetheless, and with all allowances made for the subtleties and complexities of religious allegiance in the period, in the context of English history Southwell remains an eccentric, even strange figure, isolated from his contemporaries, including many of his Catholic contemporaries, by his choice of profession, belief, and death. A book about

Southwell must confront his strangeness. To paraphrase Shakespeare's Malvolio, some are born martyrs, some choose martyrdom, and some have martyrdom thrust upon them. Robert Southwell chose martyrdom; his death was the consummation of his short life's work, the realization in life of the substance of his writing. Southwell made the decision, in some ways an extremely arrogant one, to be one of the absolutely excluded. He challenged his society to kill him, and in doing so to enact publicly its own violence and illegitimacy. The effect, indeed the intention, of Southwell's work and life, was by violence to turn the world upside down in the spirit of the strongest of gospel paradoxes and reversals—in the words of the Magnificat, to put down the mighty from their seat, and to exalt the humble (Luke 2.53). The result, both as literature and life, is, to say the least problematic. Without attempting to confine Southwell to a thesis, in this book I suggest some of the issues raised by his peculiar, indeed unique, literary career.

Quotations from Southwell and other writers are presented in modernized spelling. Biblical quotations in English are from the Douay-Rheims version, which is the English version used by Southwell himself.

I would like to acknowledge the kindness of Fr. Thomas M. McCoog, S.J., in allowing me to consult his edition of the Southwell letters in the Jesuit archives, Rome, forthcoming in *Archivum Historicum Societatis Iesu.*

Chronology

1561 Robert Southwell born at Horsham St. Faith, Norfolk.

1576 Leaves England in May to receive a Catholic education abroad. Enters Jesuit school, Douai, in June; boards at the English College. Moves to the Jesuit college of Clermont, Paris, in November.

1577 Returns to Douai in June.

1578 Is refused admission to the Jesuit novitiate. Leaves Douai for Rome in summer. Enters Jesuit novitiate at Sant' Andrea 17 October and continues his studies at the Jesuits' Roman College.

1581 Completes his course in philosophy with distinction. Transfers to the English College, where he is first tutor, then prefect of studies.

1584 Is ordained a priest.

1585 In January requests to be sent to England.

1586 Leaves Rome in April. Lands in England in July and begins his underground life as a missionary priest. Late in the year, becomes chaplain to the countess of Arundel.

1587 Early in the year, composes *An Epistle of Comfort,* which is then secretly printed.

1589 Composes *An Epistle of Robert Southwell unto His Father* in October.

1591 Composes *The Triumphs over Death,* September. *Mary Magdalen's Funeral Tears* is published late in the year. Composes *An Humble Supplication to Her Majesty* at the end of the year.

1592 Completes *A Short Rule of Good Life.* Is captured 26 June in the Bellamys' house, Uxenden. After severe torture, is moved to the Tower in late July.

1595 Brought to trial 20 February for treason before the court of Queen's Bench and is convicted by reason of

	his priesthood. At Tyburn, 21 February, is hanged, drawn, and quartered. *Saint Peter's Complaint, With Other Poems* published in March. *Moeoniae, or, Certain Excellent Poems and Spiritual Hymns* published in October. *The Triumphs over Death* published.
1596–1597	*A Short Rule of Good Life* and *An Epistle of Robert Southwell unto His Father* secretly printed in England.
1970	Is canonized by Pope Paul VI 25 October. The Society of Jesus celebrates his feast on 21 February.

Chapter One

The Life and Death of Robert Southwell

Birth, Family, and Education

No record of Robert Southwell's birth survives. At his admission to the Jesuit novitiate in October 1578, he was about 17, and at his trial on 20 February 1595 he said he was about 33 years old. From these rather imprecise facts his biographers have concluded that he was born in the later part of 1561 (Janelle, 6n10; Devlin, 3, 308).

His parents were Richard and Bridget (née Copley) Southwell of Horsham St. Faith, Norfolk, and he was the third and youngest son in a family of three boys and five girls. The Southwells were a wealthy, well-connected family, prominent in the county since the fifteenth century, who owed their money to a combination of court service and judicious marriage. Robert's grandfather, Sir Richard, was an adroit, unprincipled courtier who, as a commissioner for the suppression of the monasteries, made money out of the dissolution. His house at Horsham was built in the grounds of the former Benedictine abbey of St. Faith. Unfortunately, despite powerful, even glamorous connections,[1] in Robert's father's time the Southwells lost their money through family feuds, lawsuits, and feckless investment. In the period of Robert's missionary work in England, Richard Southwell had to sell his estate, and even experienced imprisonment for debt.[2]

Robert was a studious, quiet child whose father "in merriment" called him "Father Robert"; he was brought up Catholic, because, as he later wrote, Catholicism was "by descent and pedigree . . . in manner hereditary" to his family (*Letters,* 3). When it came time to decide upon his education, like other boys of his faith and class he was sent surreptitiously out of England to school on the Continent, in his case to Douai, where William Allen had established an English residence and seminary attached to the University. The college diaries record that Mr. Southwell and Mr. Cotton, "both noblemen's sons" arrived 10 June 1576.[3] Robert was 14 years old. It would be 10 years before he returned to England,

and he never saw his parents again, unless, perhaps, his father visited him in prison in 1592.

In Douai he lodged at the English College, but attended classes at the much larger Jesuit College, a school of about a thousand pupils. In November, because of political turmoil in the Low Countries, he was sent with other boys from Douai to Paris, where he resumed his education at the Jesuit College of Clermont. It used to be thought that he stayed in Paris for two years, but according to Christopher Devlin he was there only until the following June, when he returned to Douai (Devlin, 29; Knox, 1:124). It was not long before the religious and political troubles in the Netherlands disrupted the life of the English College once again. In 1578, when Allen moved his college to Rheims to quarters provided by the Duc de Guise, Southwell stayed behind with the Jesuits; but they too were soon forced to close their schools and send their pupils and novices home. At that point Robert Southwell made the defining decision of his life; instead of returning to his parents, he went to Rome. At first he lodged at the English hospice, then in the first stages of its transformation, under Allen's influence, into the English College. But he did not stay there. In October 1578, when he was about 17 years old, Southwell entered the Jesuit novitiate and resumed his studies at the Jesuits' Roman College, later incorporated into the Pontifical Gregorian University (Devlin, 38–40).

Rome: Novice, Teacher, and Jesuit

Why did Robert Southwell as a teenaged boy enter upon the life of religion? Some answers may be found in his writing:

> The purpose of my entry is, first that by constant mortification of self, by sincere contempt of the world, and by a perfect observance of my rule and my vows I may become, as far as I can, like unto Christ who was crucified for me, and may strive with all my heart to love him: second that I may do penance in this life for the numberless sins I have committed against God: third, that mistrusting my own weakness, poverty, and ignorance, I may in all things commit myself to the authority of His ministers and representatives, and entrust to them the entire care of my soul and body: lastly, that, if the will of God, as made known to me by superiors should so ordain, I may with all my energies devote myself to the salvation of my neighbour.[4]

Those are entirely correct, impersonal reasons for becoming a Jesuit given by Southwell the novice during practice of the famous Ignatian spiritual exercises, when he had already submitted himself fully to the discipline of the order. They do not express a personal motivation, and in fact no documentation of Southwell's personal motives survives. There are, however, two documents (his *Querimonia* and a letter) showing that the decision to become a Jesuit was a hard one to make, that it dominated the difficult, passionate years of his adolescence, and that confessors, as one would expect, had a hand in it.[5] The documents also reveal that the fundamental motive was probably a kind of boyish romanticism.

Indeed, one consequence of the English government's attempts to suppress Catholicism was to invest it, for young men of Southwell's generation, with an aura of romantic adventure. One sign of this development was the appearance of circles of young aristocrats who, at great risk, acted as guides, couriers, and companions to the missionary priests. In one of his letters from England, Southwell himself describes how two young men of good family guided him, and how he traveled, disguised as a gentleman and accompanied by noble young companions, from one great house to another.[6] Another sign of the romance of Catholicism is provided by a manuscript life, preserved at Stonyhurst College, of Edward Throgmorton, a saintly young man who died at 20 in the English College, Rome, in 1582. In many ways an absurd composition, this life provides an amazing picture of a group of little boys in Elizabethan Warwickshire led by Edward to form themselves into a kind of ecclesiastical scout troop, fortifying themselves against Protestant parents and teachers, helping priests, and relieving the poor.[7] Evidently the lure of comradeship in adventure was strong, and signs of a similar romantic psychology appear in the young Southwell's two documents.

He wrote the first, his *Querimonia,* or "Complaint," after the Jesuits rejected his first application to the novitiate. (Hagiographically minded biographers attribute his rejection to youth and/or political turmoil, but it seems more likely that the Jesuits thought the teenaged Southwell immature and excitable.) This document, after a verbose expression of the author's intense disappointment, gives an extremely idealized description of the joys of life within the order as a member of a privileged cadre, united against the world, secure in the service of a perfect master (Foley, 1:305–7). The same note of comradeship sounds in the second document, a letter dated October 1580 that he wrote to his friend John Deckers, recalling the circumstances of their first meeting (Pollen 1908, 294–300). At that time, uncertain of his vocation, torn between joining the Carthusians and the Jesuits and urged by his confessor (a Jesuit) to join the latter, Southwell asked whether he could be given a friend with similar interests to whom he could talk. In response his confessor introduced him to Deckers, a Dutch boy of the same age who had already decided to be a Jesuit. As the letter says, they became inseparable companions, and Robert Southwell was secured, through the friendship, for the order. Even so, he had to wait longer for admission than did Deckers, a more stolid character.

Southwell seems to have understood that longing for comradeship in a common cause, and pleasure in the affection that accompanied it, underlay much of his desire to be a Jesuit. Under the probing discipline of his formation, that knowledge evidently troubled him. In his sole surviving holograph manuscript, a collection of papers from his Roman days, there is a little essay asking whether his regret over the loss of a charming, handsome friend is "a motion of true charity, or a passion of fancy";[8] and in the letter to Deckers he is careful to end by saying that the result of their friendship, that is, membership in the society, erases its human origins: "The charity . . . which by the seal of the Holy Ghost was impressed upon us, as though in a second baptism at our entrance into the Society, so far from being at variance with true friendship, extinguishes any lurking affection arising from flesh and blood, while it fosters, increases, and perfects that which comes from God." Thus Southwell the Jesuit sought to transform the experience of Southwell the schoolboy into the materials of his new life in religion.

The suppression of personal motives and affections, even of natural feeling, was fundamental to the formation of a Renaissance Jesuit in the military discipline of the new order. In fact, like other, more conventional military organizations, the Jesuits insisted that aristocratic novices like Southwell spend a lot of time working in the kitchen of the novitiate. Throughout his *Spiritual Exercises,* a kind of devotional diary kept by the young Southwell at this period of his life, he continually exhorts himself to submit his will entirely to his superiors, to make no plans for himself, to show no preference for one person over another, to let no one know that he considers himself someone else's equal, and never to think of himself except with absolute humility so that, as he told himself at the outset, "I might become as like to my crucified Saviour as I could." Reflecting upon himself after taking his vows, he wrote, "Of all the things that are in thee or may be in thee or concern thee in any way, thou mayest for the future call nothing thine own, neither thy memory, thine intellect nor thy will" (*Exercises,* 54, 68–69, 34, 84, 60).

Inhumanly severe as this regime sounds, its ultimate aim was never merely ascetic, its effect (on Southwell at least) never souring. Its purpose was always to redirect the novice's natural gifts and his capacity for emotion outward from the self towards the service of others. Every day, Southwell tells himself, he must practice interior and exterior cheerfulness, be composed and moderate in everything, hide distress of mind under a cheerful expression, and be kind and gracious to everyone. One result of such discipline in Southwell's case was exquisite courtesy: "When thou art talking with anyone and there may be reason to suspect that thou dost not enjoy thy conversation with him or wouldst more gladly speak with another, take the greatest care not to turn thine eyes in the direction of that other. Speak not of him nor introduce his name abruptly into the conversation, but talk to thy companion, whoever he may be, as to Christ, and do violence to thine own inclination, for it is better to do good without relish, than with delight to do what is less good or even evil" (*Exercises,* 70).

One's final impression of Southwell as a formed Jesuit is of a personality that has become a carefully formed work of art: as his fellow Jesuit John Gerard said of him, "He was so wise and good, gentle and loveable."[9] One should not be surprised, therefore, that a man who expended such disciplined art upon his own life should practice an analogous art in prose and poetry, or that he should aim through literature and through example to introduce his art to his readers. In Southwell's mind, true art imitates the art of the creator, and is therefore a transforming, redeeming art. "Passions I allow, and loves I approve," he told Dorothy Arundell in the epistle to *Mary Magdalen's Funeral Tears,* "only I would wish that men would alter their object and better their intent." In so wishing to transform and incorporate the natural life into the regenerate life of religion, Southwell showed himself to be not only a Jesuit but, like his order itself, very much a product of Renaissance humanism and its passion for education.

Southwell remained at the novitiate until 1581. In that year, after completing the first part of his academic training, the philosophy course, with a distinguished public defense, he was transferred to the English College. There he became first tutor, then prefect of studies, and finally prefect of the sodality of the Blessed Virgin. He continued his own studies in theology at the Jesuit College, but he now lived in the English College as one of the staff.

The English college originated as a hospice for English pilgrims. Legend associated its founding with Ine, king of Wessex, but in fact it was a medieval foundation whose first deed dates from 1362. Funding from England ceased in 1534, and by the time of Elizabeth I very few pilgrims came from England to visit the hospice. In 1565 Dr. Morris Clynog, a Welshman, became warden, with a party of Marian refugee priests in residence. William Allen, however, who founded the seminary at Douai in 1568, thought that the hospice should either become a college or that its funds should be used elsewhere. Eventually Allen's wish that it become a college prevailed, and with an advance party from Douai in residence it began accepting students under instruction from the cardinal-protector of England in 1576. Its first prefect of studies and procurator were Jesuits, borrowed from a rather reluctant Jesuit father-general by the pope. From the beginning, though, the college suffered from internal quarrels. A national feud between English and Welsh students led to the removal of the Welsh rector and his replacement by an Italian Jesuit, Agazzari, who was the English students' choice. This appointment proved to be a very good one, but it played into the hands of those who suspected the Jesuits of wanting "to capture all the English colleges as soon as they were founded," as one disgruntled Welshman said. Also, like the other English off-shore foundations, the Roman college was always a focus for the activities of English spies and agitators, and college squabbles provided them with rich material for trouble-making (Beales, 42–45).

As a Jesuit teacher and administrator at the college, Southwell found himself in the thick of the college's troubles; being prefect of studies and of the sodality, he provided a natural focus for accusations of academic favoritism and of Jesuit spying on students. (Sodalities of the Virgin became universal at Jesuit schools, their membership limited to prospective Jesuits. The college's sodality was confirmed at the first visitation, and a non-Jesuit parallel sodality founded [Beales, 122].) An enquiry into the college's affairs under Pope Sixtus V vindicated the Jesuits' administration. Nonetheless, Devlin believes that the college's troubles caused Southwell great misery, reflected in some of the later passages of his *Spiritual Exercises.* Fortunately, to judge from the letters his former students and associates sent him, the rector, Agazzari, seems to have been an exceptionally nice, able man. "I recall at times," Southwell wrote the rector from England, 22 December 1586, "the troubles you have had in the college, and in recalling them, I marvel that the devil should be able to stir up dissension among those, who here live in perfect harmony both with us and among themselves. Here, forsooth, we have so many enemies in common, that there is no time for internal factions . . . Be patient, dear Father, with our shortcomings, if occasionally the breath of storms ruffle your sea."[10]

Quite apart from his administrative and personal troubles there, Southwell's years at the English College must have been very busy. In 1584 he was ordained a priest. Then, in addition to his own studies and teaching, he evidently wrote newsletters from the college, including the *Annual Letters.* "Tell Robert not to spend so much time in writing newsletters, but to get on with his studies," Robert Persons wrote in one of his own letters.[11] Most interestingly of all, from the standpoint of this study, he began to practice his own writing in this period. One of his former students, a man called John Pitts, remembered him in his book, *De illustris Angliae scriptoribus (On the Illustrious Writers of England)*, published in 1619. Pitts claimed to have been Southwell's friend, and remembered him as a good student in philosophy and theology. He then added, "He also wooed with considerable eagerness the graces of the mother tongue both in prose and verse" (Devlin, 58).

Besides the daily life of the novitiate and later of the English College, Southwell had all around him the life of Rome during the pontificate of Gregory XIII, author of the reformed Gregorian calendar, founder of the Gregorian University, and pope at a time when, as Devlin writes, the conversion of the world really seemed possible. During Gregory's pontificate the first Japanese Christians came to Rome with their Jesuit tutors, and the great Jesuit church, the Gesù, one of the most splendid monuments of baroque Rome, was consecrated. Robert Southwell would almost certainly have been present at the consecration.

England and the Mission

Throughout Southwell's time at the college, his mind continually reverted to England. "I have been wondering which would be better," he wrote in one of the later passages of his *Spiritual Exercises,* which probably refers to his sense of a vocation for the English mission, "to manifest my desire, after prayer, to my superior, so that he may decide whether it be from God or not, or to leave the whole matter absolutely to the disposition of God" (*Exercises,* 94). Although he would have known that his superiors were reluctant to release so valuable a man to virtually certain death, he eventually made his request, in February 1585, in a letter to Aquaviva, the Jesuit father-general: "There is nothing I desire more, or that can possibly be more grateful to me in this life, than, as may seem good to your Paternity, that I may expend my labours at present upon the English; the more so as it seems, under Divine inspiration and by promise of the English themselves, the highest hope of martyrdom" (Foley, 1:318).[12] When Allen and Persons asked for him, Aquaviva released him. On 8 May 1586, he and Henry Garnet left Rome on the first stage of their journey to England.

They reached the Low Countries by late June. At Douai, Southwell met his friend Deckers again; then he and Garnet made their way to St. Omer. At that stage of the journey, and for reasons of security, even they did not know the port they would sail from. Nevertheless, news of their approach had already been sent from Paris to Sir Francis Walsingham (the Elizabethan equivalent of a director of intelligence) in England. Eventually, they were directed to Boulogne, and there, on 15 July, they received their sailing orders, and Southwell wrote a last letter, "from the threshold of death":

> Stay me, therefore, my Father, with the flowers of prayer, which ascend in the odour of sweetness; encompass me with the apples of works, that if I must needs faint, it may not be from fear, but love. If I should be in the happy choir of martyrs, were it the least among them (a thing I dare not hope, yet I vehemently desire), I will not be, God willing, unmindful of those who now remember me . . . Plead, therefore, my Father (perhaps I now address you for the last time), plead with the Common Father and Lord Jesus my cause—nay, your cause, and that of the whole Church, that I may so sustain it, representing it as I do, that I may faithfully and courageously accomplish that which God, the angels and superiors, demand of me, even should it be at the cost of life and blood itself.[13]

The first sentence quoted paraphrases Canticles 2.5, "Stay me up with flowers, compass me about with apples: because I languish with love." The love implied by the text must be the love of Christ, which is leading him to his death. Christopher Devlin, himself a Jesuit, traces the desire for martyrdom that animated Southwell's life and writing back to his Jesuit training. "At the heart of [the Jesuit discipline] there is an element of supernatural wildness expressed in [Ignatius'] famous rule, 'to recoil from everything that the world loves and embraces: to allow and long for, with the whole heart, whatever Christ Our Lord loved and embraced'" (Devlin, 85). It is hardly surprising that the English government was afraid of men disciplined to love Christ all the way to Calvary.

Even the most severe laws, administered by the most brutal torturers and judges, could not deter them.

Southwell and Garnet landed somewhere between Dover and Folkstone on 17 July (7 July by the unreformed English calendar), and made their separate ways into London, where they met a few days later.

The England to which they returned was an extremely dangerous place to be a Catholic. The merciless severity of the successive penal laws against the practice of Catholicism is evidence itself that, challenged by the success of the missionaries from Douai and Rome, the government was determined to eradicate Catholicism in England. Under the act of 1581, to be reconciled to the Church, that is, if one were Catholic, to go to confession or attend a mass, or, if one were Protestant, to be converted, became treason, and carried the death penalty for the person reconciled as well as for anyone concerned in his reconciliation. The same statute imposed enormous financial penalties for not attending the state church, and provided that the fines so levied were to be divided three ways: a third to the Crown, a third to the Crown for poor relief—and a third to the informer. Under the statute of 1585, it was made treason merely to be a seminary priest or a Jesuit in England, or to assist a priest in any way. In 1593 a further act would confine Catholics within a five-mile radius of their homes, in effect interning them in their own towns and villages.[14] Christopher Devlin estimated that in 1586, the year of Southwell's arrival in England, a priest's chance of survival was one in three. Southwell survived six years.

The task that Garnet's and Southwell's superiors had given them was an extremely difficult one. It was not merely a question of bringing the sacraments to enclaves of isolated Catholics, but of creating an organization for doing so. English Catholicism had proved to be a far tougher growth than the Protestant government expected—probably more from dislike of the new order than from any specifically religious enthusiasm—but although Catholic sentiment could survive virtually anywhere, a Catholic priest could only survive in a protected place. Consequently nearly all the missionaries lived as chaplains in houses belonging to the nobility and gentry, and, except for the Jesuits, without any kind of local ecclesiastical supervision or discipline. Some localities, therefore, were well served, while others, sometimes entire counties, never saw a priest. It was Garnet's job as superior of his two-man mission to remedy this state of affairs. His first arrangement was to station Southwell in London, while he went out into the countryside to find centers of support and communication.

Southwell first found help and protection in the household of William, third baron Vaux of Harrowden, at Hackney, a village just outside London. This arrangement soon ended with the arrests made in the wake of the Babington Plot against Elizabeth I in the late summer of 1586; in fact, Southwell himself had a very near escape during this period, described in his letter of 21 December (Pollen 1908, 313): "Twice I was in extreme danger. The pursuivants were raging all around, and seeking me in the very house where I was lodged. I heard them threatening and breaking woodwork and sounding the walls to find hiding places; yet, by God's goodness, after four hours' search they found me not, though separated from them only by a thin partition rather than a wall. Of a truth the house was in such sort watched for many nights together that I perforce slept in my clothes in a very strait, uncomfortable place." Devlin believes this happened at Lord Vaux's house. Then, towards the end of the year, through intermediaries, he received an invitation to visit the countess of Arundel, and thus began the most important relationship of his mission.

Philip Howard, earl of Arundel, was the son of the third duke of Norfolk, executed in 1572 in connection with the Ridolphi plot, and grandson to the poet Henry Howard, earl of Surrey. Arundel had been a prominent figure at Elizabeth I's court until he reverted to Catholicism, the religion of his family, and returned to his neglected wife, Anne.[15] In 1585 he attempted to cross to Europe, but was arrested and imprisoned in the Tower of London. He never left the Tower, and never saw his wife and children again.[16] When Southwell met the countess, she was living a kind of premature widowhood, probably in Arundel House on the Strand (Howard House having been lost to the Arundels with his arrest). According to her seventeenth-century biographer, in inviting Southwell she had not intended to acquire a chaplain. In the event, though, she provided him with a place to live, and it must have been through her that he acquired the printing press mentioned by Father John Gerard, which printed his first English prose work, *An Epistle of Comfort.* Devlin believes that Southwell's residence and chaplaincy with the countess ended in 1590 when Lord Hunsdon moved into Arundel House, and evicted her. Nancy Pollard Brown, however, argues that Arundel House would never have provided safe shelter for Southwell. Instead, she suggests that the countess provided Southwell with a house in Spitalfields outside the walls near Bishopsgate, within the precinct of the former Augustinian hospital. Here there was an enclave of East Anglian families who, like the Southwells, had ties to the Howards, and Brown believes that Southwell retained the use of the house until his arrest.[17]

Southwell spent much, probably most, of his time in England in the ordinary work of a priest. "I am devoting myself to sermons, hearing confessions, and other priestly duties," he wrote to Aquaviva a few weeks after his arrival (Pollen 1908, 309). Then, once he was established with a base of his own, he became a contact for newly arrived priests, whom he would supply with food, clothing, and money. He found the work demanding and intensely satisfying, despite the constant danger and the hair-breadth escapes. As he wrote, in the passionate language of Counter-Reformation piety, "That sacred blood is still warm, those wounds still open, and those bruises may still be seen, with which God redeemed the souls that we are tending. At such a sight dangers may well be scorned, lest such precious pearls be lost" (Pollen 1908, 313). Yet the fundamental challenge remained: how could so few priests reach so many souls? He told Agazzari, back at the English College, that every priest was useful, but that preachers especially were needed: "It is most important that the students should practise themselves, so as to acquire readiness of speech and a plentiful supply of matter" (Pollen 1908, 318). Yet even the best sermon reached a very limited audience. Only the written word, and especially the published word, could mediate between the individual priest and that large, unreached audience. When Southwell, offered a secure house and a press by the countess of Arundel, decided to spend so much of his time in writing, there can be no doubt that he was embarking on what Janelle calls an "apostolate of letters," and that his writing was an extension of his mission.

The idea did not originate with him. Among the instructions and faculties granted to Garnet and Southwell for their mission was permission for "some pamphlets to be printed for the defence of the faith and the edification of Catholics at the discretion of Father Weston" (Hicks, 355–56). (Father Weston was William Weston, the only Jesuit active in England when they arrived; they were instructed to find him and accept him as their superior. They succeeded in meeting him, but on 4 August 1586 he was captured,[18] and Garnet and Southwell were left to their own devices.) As policy, the permission to produce books was based upon the dramatic effects of Edmund Campion's and Robert Persons's publications in the mission of 1580–81 (Hughes, 3:307–8), and the Roman authorities must have had some hopes of the same tactic succeeding again. They knew that in his capacity as newsletter writer, Southwell had already shown a talent for public relations, and they also knew about his interest in writing English prose and poetry; during his Roman days Southwell would not have spent time on writing without his superiors' knowledge and permission.

In England, the decision to devote time to writing also required permission, this time from Garnet, who was Southwell's superior. This is an important point about the origins of Southwell's writing. Southwell's biographers used to imagine him living a life of virtual imprisonment, restricted to a small, remote room from which he only emerged after dark to go about his pastoral work. In circumstances like that, cut off from external contact, the decision to write would be as much a private as a pastoral one, and the image of the writer thus called to mind would be the conventional one of a self-motivated, solitary figure in a quiet room. It is now clear from Southwell's surviving letters that he led an active life, out and about in the world. His writing was part of that life, shared in its purpose, and was carried out under permission.

The prose works, especially, reveal their professional origins. Three of them are pastoral letters, one of the oldest of Christian prose forms. *An Epistle of Comfort* (1587), agreed to be his first prose work, originated with the idea of letters addressed to the earl of Arundel in his imprisonment. *The Triumphs over Death* (1591) is also a letter to the earl, comforting him for the death of his sister, and *An Epistle of Robert Southwell unto His Father* (1589) is an exhortation to return to the Church, addressed to his own father, Richard Southwell. According to its dedicatory epistle, Southwell's most popular prose work, *Mary Magdalen's Funeral Tears* (published 1591), was composed in response to a request. Devlin thinks that the original occasion of the request was a sermon on the subject of Mary Magdalen, but Nancy Pollard Brown is probably nearer the mark in suggesting that its recipient was planning to become a nun (Devlin, 117–18; *Letters,* xxv). *A Short Rule of Good Life* (1591?), a very practical little book, was no doubt written for a specific person, perhaps the countess of Arundel. The last work, *An Humble Supplication,* is the exception; but although it is not a pastoral work, one can be certain that Southwell would not have undertaken it without Garnet's advice and permission.

Southwell's own letters written in Latin to the Jesuit father-general and to the rector of the English College are the best witnesses to his years in England, but unfortunately they are hard to come by. There is no complete list of them, let alone a complete edition; they survive in a wide variety of sources, and currently available texts and translations are unreliable.[19] Maintaining correspondence between England and the

Continent was dangerous and difficult; because letters were often intercepted or lost, the writers tended to be discreet, speaking either in generalities or using code language. Merchants and commerce, for instance, offered an easy metaphorical code for discussing the news of the mission, as when Southwell wrote to Persons in 1582, shortly after Edmund Campion's execution, "I am so glad to hear how well Ours have comported themselves, especially he with whom you started [Edmund Campion] . . . He has had the start of you in loading his vessel with English wares, and has successfully returned to the desired port" (Pollen 1908, 302). Southwell's later letters from England, however, are comparatively plainspoken—in fact Aquaviva rebuked him for being indiscreet in his first letters. His old habits as a newsletter writer and publicist persisted, and he often wrote simply to get the news from England out into Europe. One of his most powerful letters provides an account of the pogrom against Catholics that followed the Spanish Armada, and one of his last surviving letters gives an account of the treatment of Catholic prisoners that was prophetic of his own fate: "Some are hung for whole days by the hands so that they can just touch the ground with the tips of their toes. Truly, anyone imprisoned there is 'in the pit of misery and the mire of dregs.' The one purgatory we all fear is the place where Topcliffe and Young, those two executioners of Catholics, have freedom to torture."[20]

Capture, Torture, and Imprisonment

Richard Topcliffe, "an atrocious psychopath" in the phrase of the contemporary poet Geoffrey Hill, "homo sordidissimus" ("a most vile man") in Father Garnet's words, was a foreseeable consequence of the penal laws against Catholicism;[21] in fact his development into a figure of power began soon after the passage of the 1585 act. In 1586 he appeared as "her majesty's servant," and seems never to have held any other official title; indeed, his relationship to the queen is mysterious. His letters to her reveal that he enjoyed some of the privileges of a favorite, including ready access, and he bragged to Father Thomas Pormort about the intimate familiarities she allowed him (Pollen 1908, 210). He seems to have been able to bypass the Privy Council, and address the queen directly. His business was hunting Catholics, and he was so well-known for it that about the court "topcliffizare" meant "to hunt a recusant." To help him in his business he operated a kind of private army, and he enjoyed rights of arrest, imprisonment, and torture under various warrants from the Privy Council. His first serious setback, in 1594, illustrates the Topcliffian method. An associate, Thomas Fitzherbert, had bound himself to pay Topcliffe £5000 if Topcliffe would persecute to death his father and uncle and a Mr. Bassett. When Fitzherbert failed to pay up, arguing that the conditions had not been met because his relations died naturally, Topcliffe sued. At the private hearing of this extraordinary case, Topcliffe insulted some privy councilors; when, in consequence, he found himself in the Marshalsea prison for contempt of court, he wrote directly to the queen for assistance.[22]

In January 1592, a woman called Anne Bellamy, daughter of a Catholic family who lived at Uxenden outside London, was committed to the Gatehouse prison for recusancy. There Topcliffe either seduced or raped her. As part of a complicated scheme to marry her off with a dowry to a henchman of his, she was persuaded to lure Southwell to her family's house, thus betraying her family and the priest simultaneously on Topcliffe's promise (unkept) that her family would not be harmed. On 25 June, Southwell set out from London for Uxenden with her brother Thomas. Arrived at the house, he celebrated a mass and preached to a large congregation of family and tenants. That night, Topcliffe and his private army broke into the house, and captured Southwell, whom he took back to his private house in Westminster the next morning. He then wrote to the queen a letter asking permission to torture Southwell:

> I have presumed (after my little sleep) to run over this examination enclosed, faithfully taken and of him foully and suspiciously answered, and somewhat knowing the nature and doings of the man, may it please your majesty to see my simple opinion. Constrained in duty to utter it.
>
> Upon this present taking of him it is good forthwith to enforce him to answer truly and directly and so to prove his answers true in haste, to the end that such as be deeply concerned in his treacheries have not time to start or make shift.
>
> To use any means in common prisons either to stand upon or against the wall (wherein above all things exceeds, and hurteth not) will give warning. But if your Highness' pleasure be to know anything in his heart, to stand against the wall, his feet standing upon the ground and his hands put as high as he can reach against the wall, like a trick at trenchmore, will enforce him to tell all, and the truth proved by the sequel . . . So humbly submitting myself to your majesty's directions in this, or in any service with any hazard, I cease until I hear your pleasure.[23]

What followed is unusually well-documented by newsletters from Richard Verstegan (who disseminated English Catholic news to the

Continent from Antwerp)[24] and Henry Garnet. Robert Southwell was tortured 40 hours in Topcliffe's house, and said not a word. Garnet later wrote that Sir Robert Cecil, who was present at the later tortures, told another gentleman "that they had a new kind of torture, no less cruel than the rack, and such that no man could bear it; and yet he had seen Robert Southwell, being thus suspended, remain as dumb as a tree-stump; and it had not been possible to make him utter one word" (Janelle, 66–67). The attraction of the hanging torture was that it was simple, and left no outward mark: "gyves, with a point pressing on the wrist, were fitted to the victim, and he was simply left to hang."[25] Prolonged much beyond 10 minutes, such hanging, like crucifixion, causes severe internal injury, then death. The torturer's skill lay in maximizing the pain while keeping the prisoner alive by letting the feet intermittently transmit some of the weight to the floor or a stool. Topcliffe almost killed Southwell by hanging him with his feet strapped to his thighs; when they took him down he vomited blood (Petti, 52).

When Topcliffe's methods produced no results, the queen turned Southwell over to the Privy Council. William Wade, a clerk to the council, and himself a notable torturer, had Southwell moved to the Gatehouse prison, where members of the council took part in the interrogations. When more torture produced none of the information they wanted—details about himself and his priesthood, the people to whom he had ministered, the names of priests in England with their whereabouts—he was left, hurt, starving, covered with maggots and lice, to lie in his own filth. Then, about a month later, at the end of July, by order of the Privy Council he was moved to solitary confinement in the Tower. According to the early narratives, his father petitioned the queen that if his son had deserved death under the law, he should so suffer, but if not, that he should be treated as a gentleman; and that as his father he should be allowed to provide his son with the necessities of life. No documentary evidence of the petition survives, and the accounts vary as to whether it came before the move to the Tower or not. Nonetheless, something of the kind must have happened, because his friends were allowed to provide him with the means of food and clothing, and to send him a Bible and the works of St. Bernard. Henry Garnet was later able to smuggle a breviary to him.

He remained in the Tower for two and a half years. From time to time the authorities interrogated him, but humanely, and evidently never with any usable result. It began to look as though he would never be brought to trial (which proved to be the case with his fellow-Jesuit, William Weston, interned at Wisbech castle), and there began to be talk of a ransom and banishment. Yet only eight months after his imprisonment, Southwell himself wrote to Sir Robert Cecil a letter asking, in effect, either to be released or brought to trial and sentenced, and providing the information they had failed to acquire by torture: that he was a Catholic priest and a Jesuit.

When Topcliffe originally captured Southwell, he asked him who he was, and Southwell replied that he was a gentleman; then, when Topcliffe accused him of being a priest and a traitor, Southwell answered that he must prove it (Petti, 67–68). Southwell's refusal, under torture, to identify himself meant that neither he nor the family that harbored him could be indicted for treason, and he persisted in maintaining silence until he heard that the government had used Anne Bellamy's testimony against her parents (something Southwell never thought would happen). He wrote to Cecil because, although his silence could no longer protect the Bellamys, it could injure the priesthood and his order if it were interpreted as evidence of either fear or shame. "I have here sent you a sharp sword," he wrote to Cecil, ". . . If it shall please you to draw and to use it, the hand that sent it hath a heart to endure it" (*Letters,* 83).[26] Even so, having this information, the government waited two years before acting. Did they hope that Southwell, seriously injured for life by torture, would simply die? The story of his sufferings and his courage was well-known, and there was no wish to make another martyr, and besides, as Janelle writes, Southwell's "gentle birth, commanding personality and literary fame, his obvious guiltlessness of any hateful offence compelled them to a show of humaneness" (Janelle, 84–85). On the other hand, the sudden decision to try him in February 1595 puzzled observers at the time, and no good reason for it has been found since. The government must have had reason to believe that a trial would discredit him.

Trial and Conviction

On 18 February 1595, Southwell was transferred to Newgate prison to await trial. He remained there three days in the notorious underground cell nicknamed Limbo, but found it furnished for him by the kindness of the keeper and a friend with bed, fire, and candles. On 20 February he was taken to Westminster to the Court of Queen's Bench to be tried by Lord Chief Justice Popham and other justices under the statute of 1585, which made it treason to be a Catholic priest in England. Sir Edward Coke, attorney-general, presented the government's case, and Topcliffe was also present. Southwell himself was still very weak. According to Garnet, he asked a friendly jailer to stay near him "in case some accident should happen to him, or he should be in need of anything, because (as a result of his bitter tortures) his sides were not strong enough to shout" (Devlin, 294).

There are two eyewitness accounts of the trial and subsequent execution, one of unknown authorship, the other by a priest, Thomas Leake. Leake's account is the sketchier, but the two agree in the main points, thus showing us what impressed the spectators most.[27] Although the legal verdict was a foregone conclusion, the drama of the trial clustered about three themes. The first was the legitimacy of the proceeding itself. The trial began with the reading of the indictment, which simply stated that, being a priest, Southwell "traitorously . . . was and remained" at Uxenden, contrary to the statute. Instructed to plead, Southwell asked if he might speak. No, he was told, he must either confess the indictment or plead not guilty. Southwell then answered that he was a Catholic priest, and that it was no use denying he had been at Uxenden, for the whole household had seen him; he intended no treason, but only to administer the sacraments to those willing to receive them. "Mr. Southwell," said Popham again, "you must answer, and either confess the indictment, or say 'Not guilty.'" Southwell answered, "Not guilty of any treason."

A similar duel followed over the conventional question, "How will you be tried?" To this Southwell answered, "By God and you," and the chief justice again told him, "You must answer directly, for we are not to try you, but the law." To this Southwell answered again that he would be tried by God and them, "for the laws were not according to the word of God." Then Popham told him, rather wearily one suspects, that he must "put himself upon trial by God and the country, otherwise refusal was a sufficient condemnation." Having made his point, Southwell replied that he was loath that the poor jurors should be "accessory, or guilty to his death," but that if the court "will needs have it treason that I must lay upon the jury, I will be tried by God and the country."

In this way Southwell defended himself, not against the inevitable verdict, but in the eyes of the spectators, by challenging the legitimacy of the court and of the law under which he was being tried. Another dramatic moment, noticed in both accounts, occurred in the opening stages of the trial as the attorney-general was developing his case. There were three points to the indictment, he said: first, the prisoner was a subject "born within this land"; second, he was made a priest by the authority of Rome; and third, he was at Uxenden on the day in question. All of these would be proved. "I know he will and must confess it likewise that he was made a priest since the first year of her majesty's reign, for he was born since her majesty's reign, which he also acknowledged." At that moment Popham interrupted to ask Southwell how old he was, "seeming to scorn his youth." Southwell replied "that he was near about the age of our Saviour, who lived upon the earth thirty-three years; and he himself was as he thought near about thirty-four years." This reply produced an outraged protest from Topcliffe that Southwell had compared himself to Christ. "No," said Southwell, "I am a humble worm created by Christ." Nonetheless, with his first answer he made explicit an analogy between the proceedings and the trial of Christ that was always present to the minds of sympathetic spectators at priests' trials. A few moments later, when Attorney-general Coke told the court that the act of 1585 made it treason to be a priest in Uxenden, Southwell replied that he knew the act, but that it was impossible for such a law to be agreeable to the word of God.

That statement made Coke angry enough to depart from his planned speech in order to justify the law, and when Southwell tried in his enfeebled voice to argue the point he was told to keep silent until the attorney-general had finished. This led Southwell to introduce the second theme of the trial, the inhumanity of the proceedings, when he begged that he might answer immediately: "because he could not carry it so well in mind, by reason that his memory and senses were much impaired through Mr. Topcliffe's means, under whose hands he protested of his soul, and as he expected very shortly to answer it before Almighty God, he had been ten times tortured so extremely that the least of them was worse than ten executions."

Popham and Coke denied knowledge of the torture, Coke with an equivocation, "that he never knew he was racked," and Topcliffe with an evasion, that Southwell was never upon the rack. When Southwell told them they had tortures worse than the rack, and began to describe them, Popham cut him off, saying that torture was lawful and used in all nations, to which Southwell assented; but when he added that he wished "there might be some measure there lest a man in the end by extremity of pain, be driven to desperation," he exasperated them so much that they demanded, "Show the harm you have had by your tortures." "Let a woman show her throes," Southwell replied, an answer which so illustrated the barbarity of the proceedings and his own focus on the human issues at stake that Topcliffe lost control of himself, and began to justify, excuse, and in effect confess his actions. Coke attempted to save face for the Crown by a kind of bullying bluff, saying that Topcliffe had no need to excuse his proceedings, and that, "We will tear your hearts out of a hundred of your bodies"; but Southwell was not to be deflected. There was no more barbarous a man than Topcliffe in all Christendom, he said, whereupon "Topcliffe was very earnest, and began to rail, but they would not permit him."

The third theme, equivocation, was the Crown's, and with it Coke undoubtedly hoped to turn sympathy in the courtroom against the prisoner. He called his sole witness, Anne Bellamy, now Mrs. Nicholas Jones, who testified that Southwell had taught her that if she were asked upon oath whether she had seen a priest or not, if she had, then she could lawfully answer no, reserving to herself the meaning that she had seen no one with intent to betray him. This was the first appearance in an English court of the notorious doctrine of equivocation. Coke presented his evidence as if Southwell had been teaching his penitents to lie under oath, whereas in fact the case was exactly opposite; equivocation was a means of speaking under oath without either lying or incriminating oneself. As Devlin observes, both the Puritans and the Catholics who used equivocation did so because "they were up against a system of forced self-accusation . . . and they would not allow lies." The government, on the other hand, was horrified and alarmed because "the chief weapon of Tudor law, self-accusation, was being countered by the older and banished principle . . . that no man is bound to incriminate himself" (Devlin, 301–2).

Southwell's only comment on the evidence itself was that it did not represent accurately what he had said. He then tried to argue the subtleties of the subject, but found himself continually interrupted and shouted down. Eager to defend himself against the very serious and unexpected charge of teaching lying, he therefore turned the accusation against attorney Coke himself, telling him that he could only reject his teaching at the cost of proving himself "no good subject, nor friend of the queen." According to the eyewitness's account, Coke allowed himself to accept the challenge, perhaps out of vanity. Southwell then put a hypothetical case: suppose the French invaded England, and the queen were forced to take refuge in Attorney-General Coke's house; suppose he were taken, and put upon oath to tell where she was; and suppose Mr. Attorney refused to swear, and his refusal was taken as an admission that she was in the house; should he swear or not? "If," Southwell concluded, "Mr. Attorney refused to swear that her Majesty were not there, with this intention, not to tell them, then I say Mr. Attorney were neither her majesty's good subject nor friend."

Popham said that Coke should not swear. "Then," said Southwell, "that were by silence to betray his sovereign." Coke had no answer except insults. Popham, his mind engaged, apparently, for the first time in the trial, said that "if this doctrine be allowed, it would supplant all justice, for we are men, and no gods, and can judge but according to their outward actions and sayings, and not according to their secret and inward intuitions." Southwell attempted to meet this objection by pointing out that in all such cases, including his hypothetical one, everything depends upon the nature of the oath and the authority of the questioner; but being continually interrupted, he desisted, asking them to bear with him, since they would not allow him to prove what he had said. With that the trial ended, though not without more outbursts from Topcliffe.

The jurors brought in a verdict of guilty according to the indictment. Asked whether he had anything to say, Southwell answered, "I pray God forgive all them that any way are accessory to my death." Even now, Topcliffe broke in, saying he had found Southwell hiding under the tiles among his gods (i.e., religious articles), with Persons's code. With the trial over and the verdict in, Southwell must have been relieved, even happy, and he turned from Topcliffe with a joke, that it was time to hide when Mr. Topcliffe came. After a long speech, which seems to have been yet another rehearsal of the Crown's case (to which once again, Southwell was not permitted to reply), Popham pronounced the appalling sentence: "that he should be carried to Newgate whence he came, and from thence to be drawn to Tyburn upon a hurdle, and there to be hanged and cut down alive; his bowels to be burned before his face; his head to be stricken off; his body to be quartered and disposed at her majesty's pleasure." After which, the witness writes, "Mr. Southwell made thereunto a low and humble reverence, and gave great thanks for it." The trial over, the officers then escorted Southwell through the streets to Newgate, having decided "he would go quiet enough," and so he enjoyed a kind of quiet triumph as he passed between lines of friends and well-wishers, who judged themselves "happy to obtain one glance from him." Some Protestant ministers are said to have visited him in prison, but the government never made public what passed between them.[28]

Death

As with the trial, so with the execution: the two firsthand accounts corroborate each other where they overlap, although *A Brief Discourse* provides more detail than Thomas Leake. Both begin with Southwell's being laid upon the hurdle, Leake saying that he was laid upon straw, with a cord fastened about his wrists.[29] Both agree that as the hurdle was drawn along, Southwell was intent upon mental prayer and meditation, keeping his head, hands, and eyes raised towards heaven as much as he could. "He used not any speech," wrote Leake, "but was drawn *tanquam ovis ad occisionem,* as a sheep to the slaughter." *A Brief Discourse* adds that an old countryman persisted in calling out, "God in heaven bless and strengthen you," despite being rebuked for it; also that a kinswoman approached the hurdle to greet him and ask for his prayers. He thanked her, asking for her prayers in return; then he warned her to be careful of the horses (either because they might hurt her, or spatter her with mud), and advised her to leave in case she should be arrested. On approaching Tyburn, "He somewhat raised himself up to behold it joyfully, and laid him down again." Once arrived at the place of execution, they took him off the hurdle and led him to the cart, where he stood a little while, wiping his mouth and face clean of the grime of the streets with a handkerchief, which he threw towards someone he recognized. Then, when the hangman pulled him into the cart, and began to open his doublet, he asked permission to speak, and receiving it began in Latin, "If we live, we live in God; if we die, we die in God; whether we live or die, we are God's"; but as soon as he said, "I am brought hither to die . . ." the under-sheriff interrupted him, telling him, "he should only cry God's mercy, and make an end."

As at his trial, Southwell persisted, asking permission once more, saying that he would deliver nothing offensive to the queen or the state; and so, receiving it, he began again with, "I am come hither to play out the last act of this poor life." Although the accounts differ slightly in the order and detail of the speech, they agree upon its contents: that he asked forgiveness of his sins, and that he prayed for the queen and the country. They agree, too (although they place it differently), that he referred to his death, saying that although it might seem disgraceful in the eyes of the world, it was honorable before God. At some point during the speech, one of the ministers present (the chaplain of the Tower, according to Leake) objected to his words about salvation, and interrupted him; but the people shouted to the minister to be quiet, and

Southwell, saying that he hoped to be saved by the merits of his Savior, simply asked the minister not to trouble him. He finished by saying that he died a Catholic priest in the Roman faith, and asking all Catholics present to pray for him. Then, as he stood in his shirt, beating his breast and repeating the liturgical words, "Into thy hands, O Lord, I commend my spirit," the cart was drawn away.

It seems that the knot had been clumsily tied so that, as *A Brief Discourse* describes, "he remained hanging alive a good space, knocking his breast, and making divers times as well as he could the sign of the cross." One of the officers, the under-sheriff again, says Leake, attempted to have him cut down alive according to the sentence; but there was a group of noblemen present, among them Lord Mountjoy, who would not allow this. The people, encouraged by the noblemen's example, shouted that he should hang until he were dead, and so the hangman pulled him downwards by the legs. Even so, it seems from both accounts that despite the good intentions of people and hangman, he was still alive when cut down.[30] The people, whose role on these occasions was to revile the sufferer, fell silent, and failed to answer the presentation of the severed head with the usual cry of "Traitor!" Instead, as Garnet wrote to Rome, they all took their hats off, so that a very angry under-sheriff told the noblemen present, "I see there are some here who have come not to honour the Queen, but to reverence a traitor!" (Devlin, 324). Lord Mountjoy's reply is in all the accounts: "I cannot judge of his religion; but pray God, whensoever I die, that my soul may be in no worse case than his."

Chapter Two

Southwell's Prose: The First Stage

An Epistle of Comfort: The Context

As Anthony Raspa has argued, the baroque world found conviction and order in the emotionally felt coherence of analogy, symbol, and metaphor.[1] In the context of English recusant experience, the priest drawn on his hurdle to Tyburn, there to be insulted and degraded, was the central figure in a reenactment of the passion and crucifixion of Christ, complete with bystanders, officials, apostles, soldiers, and faithful women. Not only were there Elizabethan Veronicas, Simons, Marys, and Josephs of Arimathea; even the executioners played their parts with a kind of headlong bravura, as in the case of the under-sheriff at Southwell's execution. All of them recognized the analogy, and whether they accepted or denied its truth, submitted themselves to the implied script, apparently conscious that these occasions demanded of them a kind of art. They put on their performances, moreover, against a background of 300 years of typological drama enacted in the streets, and only recently forbidden. Between the gospel narrative of Christ's passion and Thomas Leake's account of Southwell's death intervene the mystery plays, the Passion plays, and the Good Friday processions of pre-Reformation England. For the recusant, the mimetic principle animating play, procession, and execution alike was the same: the imitation of Christ.

When Janelle, therefore, wrote that Southwell's trial and execution "are in themselves a work of art of supreme beauty," he was responding to the disciplined sureness of Southwell's performance as a martyr (Janelle, 286–87). Compared to such mastery of the arts of living and dying, Southwell's achievements in the arts of prose and verse have seemed, especially to his co-religionists, comparatively insignificant. Yet with Southwell, perhaps more than with any other English Renaissance writer, the life and the work are inextricably involved; the writing draws its peculiarly objective strength from the same self-denying discipline that shaped the author's life and death. From the time Southwell entered the Jesuit College in Douai, his life was a preparation for martyrdom, and his writing was part of that preparation.

Among the missionary priests Southwell was unusual, not in hoping for martyrdom,[2] but in leaving such a complete record of his desire. In his *Spiritual Exercises,* under the heading, "Reflexions on St. Luke's Day after taking my vows," he wrote to himself, "Thy soul is espoused to the Crucified One and therefore thou must be crucified both in soul and body." Used in these contexts, "crucified" might at first seem metaphorical, as in an earlier passage of the *Exercises* where he wrote that the purpose of his entry into religion was to become, as far as possible, like Christ "who was crucified for me." Most readers would assume, in that case, that the likeness desired was metaphorical, not literal. Southwell's careful distinction, made on St. Luke's day, between crucifixion of soul and body suggests that that assumption would be mistaken. By crucifixion of soul, Southwell meant at least two things: the self-denial mentioned in the St. Luke's Day entry ("Thou mayest for the future call nothing thine own, neither thy memory, thine intellect nor thy will"), and the "violence" he prescribes as a remedy for the passions "and other obstacles." By crucifixion of the body, however, he meant nothing short of a painful, sacrificial death (*Exercises,* 35, 59–60).

In what one might call the form of martyrdom as it presented itself to Southwell's contemplation, crucifixion of the soul was the prelude to crucifixion of the body: "Thou shouldst ever wish and desire from thy heart to be placed among the very lowest and if possible to be esteemed as nothing. In no other manner is the way opened to martyrdom and the cross, in no other manner canst thou attain thy desire of being made like Christ crucified."[3] In a way peculiarly precise to Southwell's mind, therefore, only at the point of death does the martyr become a whole, fully realized person, when the life of inward denial and violence is finally manifested sacramentally in an outward and visible sign. Moreover, the whole meaning of the sacrament of martyrdom rests upon a conviction that in this world suffering for the love of God is the Christian's lot and a sign of God's favor. Sin is both unavoidable and the ultimate violence against God: "As St. Augustine says, it would be better that the whole world should be destroyed than that even a venial sin should be committed against God." Thus the truly happy die early; those who live are preserved either to sin or to witness in their lives and bodies the violence of sin and Satan's defeat:

> If God who knows man's misery, still wishes to lengthen my life (although He knows that it cannot be without at least venial sin), and to exercise me still further in this valley of tears, then let toil come, let come chains, imprisonment, torture, the cross of Peter and Andrew, the grid-iron of Lawrence, the flayer of Bartholomew, the lions of Ignatius, all things in a word which can possibly come. Indeed, my dearest Jesus, I pray from my heart that they may come, and by Thy wounds and the sufferings of Thy Saints, by thy merits and theirs, I most humbly beg that they may begin now at this very moment when I am writing, and last until the very end of my life. For thy sake allow me to be tortured, mutilated, scourged, slain and butchered. I refuse nothing (*Exercises,* 90, 103–4).

Not every reader of this extraordinary piece of self-typologizing will agree with Geoffrey Hill that the three words "I refuse nothing" transform "a hovering morbidity into a positive oblation" (Hill, 33). Southwell's two chief anxieties were either that his health would prevent him from enduring the torments of martyrdom, or that despite his desire and his preparation, divine providence would preserve him, as it preserved Saints Dominic and Francis, for other purposes (*Exercises,* 109). When his superiors dispatched him to England, martyrdom became a near certainty, and his first literary task there was to provide a martyr's manual for others.

The imprisonment of the Earl of Arundel offered the occasion. Although the dukedom of Norfolk was in attainder, the Earl of Arundel, as the son of the Duke of Norfolk and head of the great family of Howard, was the premier nobleman in England. Consequently, his reversion to Catholicism and subsequent capture and imprisonment had great symbolic importance for the Catholics and for the government. "It was proposed to the Earl of Arundel by the ministers of state, and I believe by the Queen herself," Southwell wrote to Aquaviva very soon after landing in England, 25 July 1586, "that if he would only consent for honor's sake to bear the sword as usual before the queen to church and there wait till the end of the service and of evensong, he should be set free." After consulting his "spiritual directors," he refused, "for his resolution is not to swerve a hair's breadth from his duty as a Catholic" (Pollen 1908, 309). As Southwell's letter suggests, keeping the earl to his resolution was immensely important to the directors of the English mission.

William Weston, S.J., had originally received the earl into the church, and then served as his chaplain. With Weston's capture in the summer of 1586, the Arundel family was left without spiritual direction. Towards the end of the year the Countess of Arundel approached Southwell through intermediaries. According to Devlin (133), she sent her gentlewoman to ask her relations in the Vaux and Arundell families whether there was a priest available to bring the sacraments to her, and they recommended Southwell. It is hard to believe that it was quite so simple and straightforward as that. If the Jesuits were to put the organization of the English mission on a proper footing, they needed an operational base that only a family with the power and influence of the Howards could provide. When one of only two Jesuits at liberty in England acquired the post of chaplain to the wife of the premier nobleman in the kingdom, there was more at stake than bringing the sacraments to the nobleman's wife.[4] Through the countess Southwell and Garnet acquired the tangible assets of a safe house, funds, and a printing press (Gerard, 26). For their propaganda war with the government, they also acquired the immensely valuable, intangible asset of the Earl of Arundel's obedience to their direction. William Weston, a priest of simple, even fanatical zeal, laid the foundations of the family's adherence to the Jesuit approach to the English mission: strict Catholic observance, and no compromise with the Protestant state. As a candidate to succeed Weston, Southwell offered three qualifications: he was a Jesuit, he was nobly born, and he had a hereditary connection with the Howards. Nonetheless, the decision to continue the Jesuit presence in the family must have been agreeable both to the network of families concerned and to Southwell's superior, Garnet. The situation of the earl, imprisoned for his religion, provided the originating idea for Southwell's *An Epistle of Comfort.*

An Epistle of Comfort: The Work

An Epistle of Comfort, Southwell's first book written on the mission, is dated by a statement in the fifteenth chapter, "You have labored to suppress us this twenty-nine years,"[5] which limits composition to 1587, the twenty-ninth year following the queen's accession (Janelle, 147). It was written, Southwell claims in "To the Reader," "to an especial friend of mine," and like other Elizabethan authors he claims to have had no intention of publishing: "the entreaty of divers, enforced me so far, that I could not but condescend to the publishing of the same, though it cost me no small labor in altering the style." Yet as Devlin argues very cogently (141–44), evidence indicates that a secret Catholic press was operating under Howard protection in early 1587, very soon after Southwell came under the Countess of Arundel's protection. The Marprelate pamphleteer who printed news of the press said that it was in Howard House itself, but Nancy Pollard Brown, after some skillful literary detective work, has located it in a house that the Countess of Arundel owned in Spitalfields (Brown 1989, 123). Consequently, one doubts Brown's statement, based on Southwell's preface, that the book was "based on letters written to console and support the countess's husband" (122–23). Time alone seems to rule out such a lengthy process of composition. What seems to have happened is that having acquired their safe house and their press, the Jesuits went into action immediately, operating under the permissions already granted by their superiors. No doubt Arundel's position, besieged as he was by arguments from both sides, occasioned the book. Perhaps there was even a letter or two written to him—but there is no reason to take Southwell's statement of authorial modesty entirely seriously. There was a strategy and a policy behind the writing and publishing of the *Epistle,* which had a much larger audience than the solitary nobleman in the Tower. Even the conventional preface, suggesting that this was an ordinary Elizabethan author, writing in a mode of the time, was part of the strategy.

It was a book whose contents Southwell had been meditating throughout his period of education and training, and its title page bore one of his favorite texts: "The kingdom of heaven suffereth violence, and the violent bear it away" (Matthew 11.12). Whatever this mysterious and paradoxical text might mean in its context,[6] something of its meaning on Southwell's title page can be gathered from his use of it in his *Spiritual Exercises,* where it follows the statement that "It is a great hindrance [to perfection] to refrain from using violence to oneself" (*Exercises,* 59). The violent who bear away the kingdom in the second part of the verse are the faithful Catholics who defeat the malice of Satan by offering to suffer in their own persons the worst that he can inflict. Christian discipline, it seems, is a countervailing violence offered to humanity's own fallen nature to prevent it from falling into enemy hands. Like his Puritan opposites, Southwell took it for granted that this life is a theater of war between good and evil, fought in the human soul and in human society. The purpose of the *Epistle* is to provide a reading of contemporary English Catholic experience according to that belief, and to prepare its readers for the very worst that can happen to them by persuading them that it is really the very best in disguise. Although he addressed the book specifically to those "restrained in durance for the Catholic faith," he seems to have conceived it with a much larger audience in mind, made up of everyone who might experience suffering in a good cause.

Of the book's 16 chapters, the first 11 are devoted to sources of comfort for the afflicted Catholics, arranged climactically, beginning with the general principle that suffering is a sign of God's favor, and culminating in a justification of martyrdom as "most profitable to the Church, and honorable to the martyrs." Each chapter is devoted to a proposition; for example, chapter 1 presents the thesis that "the first cause of comfort in tribulation is that it sheweth us to be out of the devil's power." Southwell's method of convincing his reader is predominantly emotional. He does not argue the premises of his case; instead, he cites biblical and patristic authority, and provides vivid examples and comparisons, such as the image of the ship that so appealed to Janelle (202):

> And as the ship, while it is upon the main sea, is in a manner a castle or common wealth by itself, and having all the sails hoised up, and swollen with the wind, and the banners displayed with a very lofty show, danceth upon the waves, and allureth every eye to behold the pride thereof: but when it is comen into the haven, it is straight ransacked by the searcher, forced to pay custom, and the sails being gathered, the banners taken in, the anchors cast, it lieth quietly at road and is little regarded: so they, that while they sailed upon the surges of worldly vanities, and followed the tide of a conscienceless course, might range uncontrolled, and having the favorable gale of authority to waft them forward, and honors and pomp to set them forth, were admired of the people: if they chance, by Gods calling to retire themselves into the port of true faith and virtuous life, to work their salvation, they are straight searched, and sacked, their sails gathered, the accustomed wind set, their glory disgraced, and they little or nothing esteemed (*Epistle,* 7b–8a).

Southwell's essential method, however, is that of his own Jesuit formation. Having begun modestly and generally, pointing out that suffering is a sign that his readers are out of the devil's power, and that they are loved by God, he comes with chapter 3 to the first major point of the book: in suffering we imitate Christ, and like St. Paul we need no other schooling but Christ's example: "He would have no other university but *Jerusalem,* no other school but Mount *Calvary,* no other pulpit but the *Cross,* no other reader but the *Crucifix,* no other letters but his *Wounds,* no other commas but his *Lashes,* no other full points but his *Nails,* no other book but his *open side,* and finally no other lesson but *scire Jesum Christum et hunc crucifixum:* to know Jesus Christ and him crucified" (*Epistle,* 29a). Having thus rhetoricized the wounded Christ as text for the reader's intellectual contemplation, Southwell then goes to work upon the emotions; we neglect the call of Christ, he argues, because we choose the love of earthly beauty. He creates a long, sustained image of a knight's devotion to "the fading beauty, of a fair lady's countenance," but only to destroy it: "O unspeakable blindness of man's heart, that so easily traineth to senses' lure, and is so soon caught with the beauty of an image and hath not grace to remember whom it resembleth" (*Epistle,* 35a). Finally, in a passage of extraordinary rhetorical power, he substitutes the beauty of the wounded Christ for the lady's beauty:

> Let us but consider, the last tragical pageant of his Passion, wherein he won us, and lost himself. And mark the excessive love shewed therein, which if any other than God had uttered, it would have been at the least deemed a senseless dotage, weighing by whom, and to whom it was intended. Let us view him with the eyes of our heart, and we shall (saith S. *Bernard*) discover a most lamentable sight: we shall see his head full of thorns, his ears full of blasphemies, his eyes full of tears, his mouth full of gall, his body full of wounds, his heart full of sorrow . . . O Christian, saith S. Augustine. *Ama amorem illius, qui amore tui amoris, descendit in uterum Virginis, ut ibi amorem suum amori tuo copularet.* Love the love of him, that for love of thy love, descended into the womb of a Virgin, and afterward ascended to the ignominy of the Cross, that there he might couple his love, and thy love together (*Epistle,* 38a–b).

And so, having awakened the reader's intellectual and emotional interest in the theme, Southwell performs a kind of violence upon the feelings analogous to that described in his own *Spiritual Exercises,* destroying the natural, perceptible object of human love and substituting for it an imagined object that, however pitiful, can only be grotesque or ugly to the natural eye. Nor is there a hint of a shrinking from the violently illogical logic of the substitution as he adapts Augustine's conceit, adding the phrase "and afterward ascended to the ignominy of the cross" to make the cross the marriage bed where the love of Christ and the soul is consummated. The chapter ends triumphantly, all the paradoxes in place: "Finally we are Christians, whose captain is a crucifix, whose standard the Cross, whose armor patience, whose battle persecution, whose victory death, whose triumph martyrdom."

This, in microcosm, is the method of the book: to argue a paradox with absolute seriousness, and never to flinch from the most grotesque conclusions. Having enlisted his reader under the banner of the cross, Southwell proceeds in chapters 4 and 5 to demonstrate that suffering is inseparable from human life and in most cases is no more than the sufferer deserves. The subject matter of these chapters, including a detailed description of the pains of hell, is conventional enough; nonetheless, Southwell keeps up the intellectual and emotional pressure on his reader. The prose, always exact and economical, sometimes anticipates Sir Thomas Browne, both in its subtly cadenced rhythms and in its author's enjoyment of extravagantly paradoxical behavior:

> All things therefore bending here to decay, and being tainted with death's consumption, the Saints in mourning sort, agreeably to dying and passing persons, lived in a continual farewell, as men that all ways stood upon the departure from these earthly solaces: little regarding the things that they were to leave, and having their hearts settled upon the felicity that they tended unto. And as men that at noon day desire to see the stars go down into a deep and dark well, from thence the easier to descry them: so they desiring to have the eyes of their heart perpetually fixed upon the stars of heaven, that is the glory of the Saints, descended into that profound, obscure and base kind of life, sequestering themselves from the light and pleasure of these inferior comforts, yea, and delighting in griefs, the better to conceive of future happiness. (*Epistle,* 51b–52a)

Only at the book's midpoint, having argued his reader free of attachment to this world, does Southwell turn to the peculiar situation of the imprisoned recusants and step completely into the martyr's looking-glass world in which things are their opposites: prison is freedom, violence is love, and death is life. Beginning with the argument that there is comfort and honor in suffering for the Catholic faith, he presents a series of all-too-real possibilities, starting with general persecution and ascending through imprisonment, death, and violent death to martyrdom itself.

As Helen White pointed out, Southwell's *Epistle* is a contribution to "the classic martyrological type of the encouragement to martyrdom" (1963, 249), yet it is very much a book of its own period. Southwell's persecutors are not pagan emperors, but the officers of a Christian kingdom, and only a generation earlier his imprisoned recusants would have been the persecutors of the various Protestant separatists with whom they now sometimes shared their prison space. In the England of 1587,

Southwell's triumphantly one, holy, Catholic and apostolic Church, was one of a number of competing sects. The reality of that situation had yet to dawn upon English Catholics. As John Bossy points out, although the Jesuits' organization of the English mission constituted an implicit recognition of the fact, they and most of the secular priests on the mission continued to believe in the "ideal of an all-embracing English Catholic Church . . . they were, to borrow a term from Arthur Koestler, sleepwalkers."[7] Even so, and allowing for the missioners' dream of a conversion of England, on the Catholic side as on the Protestant there was no unanimity as to what form a reestablished, reformed church should take. Insofar as the Jesuits aimed at a spiritual revival under clerical direction, they were no more likely to succeed than their Puritan counterparts in a country where the emergence of an independent, wealthy laity was the most important sociological fact of the age (Bossy, 17, 32).

On the surface, Southwell's *Epistle* is a triumphalist work taking no account of the changed realities of his country; to use Bossy's terms, Southwell recommended martyrdom for the members of the Catholic Church, not for a small, sectarian community. Nonetheless, Southwell acknowledges reality in a curiously indirect way as the tone grows increasingly controversial in the later chapters. In chapter 6, on imprisonment for the faith, he launches surprisingly crude attacks on Protestant belief and morality: "The very articles of our adversaries' religion, are of such tenor, that in reason and piety they can not be held for religious truths" (89a) and, even more absurd, "Let also the records of assizes, and sessions be searched, and let it be but shewed among so many hundred Protestants, as are yearly executed, for felonies, murders, rapes, extortions, forgeries, and such like crimes, how few recusants, have been ever in so many years, attached justly with such like offences" (92b). Chapter 12, "The unhappiness of the schismatics and lapsed," attacks Catholics who have decided to protect their families and property by compromising with the law and attending the state churches.

The effect of these controversial passages is to remove alternate voices and other claims from the arena of Catholic suffering, either the Protestant entitled to say, "I am your fellow Christian and countryman" or the "church Papist" prepared to compromise with the state and to say, "Your martyrdom is unnecessary." This isolating effect reaches a climax in chapter 13, "That heretics can not be martyrs." Virtually all the illustrative material cited to illustrate this proposition comes from the Bible and the early Church fathers, but what Southwell has in mind, of course, are the Protestant deaths of his own period, and his tone is dismissive.

On the Anabaptists: "Yet die they in defense of these damnable Paradoxes, and that with such pertinacy, as though they had bodies of steel, that felt no pain or torment. But let not this move any one to think the truth on their side" (184b). On Foxe: "But not all *Arius'* posterity, not all the races of other heretics, could maintain their doctrine, or their Martyrs' credit long, but even it fell out with them, and will do with Foxe's Martyrs, as *David* prophesied. *Vidi impium superexaltatum, et elevatum supra Cedros Libani. Et transii, et ecce non erat. Et quaesivi eum et non est inventus locus eius* [I have seen the wicked highly exalted, and lifted up like the cedars of Libanus. And I passed by, and lo, he was not: I sought him and his place was not found]" (186a).

Treated in this way, isolated from truly relevant comparisons, undefended by relevant contemporary argument, Southwell's art of martyrdom has the look of an art practiced very much for its own sake and glorying in its use of the most difficult, refractory materials to produce its most striking effects:

> But St. *Chrysostom* well saith that as the cunning artificer to abetter an image doth first melt and dissolve it; to cast it afterward in a more perfect mold: So God permitteth our flesh by you to be mangled, to make it more glorious in the second casting. And as a cunning imbroderer having a piece of torn or fretted velvet for his ground, so contriveth and draweth his work, that the fretted places being wrought over with curious knots or flowers, they far excel in show the other whole parts of the velvet: So God being to work upon the ground of our bodies, by you so rent and dismembered, will cover the ruptures, breaches and wounds, which you have made, with so unspeakable glory, that the whole parts which you left shall be highly beautified by them. (203a–b)

This is writing the body with a vengeance. With this much-quoted passage in chapter 15, "A warning to the persecutors," Southwell turns from martyrdom as the imitation of the wounded Christ to the contemplation of God as the artist crafting martyrs from the most difficult of materials, fallen humanity, and finding in the torn body of the martyr the opportunity for the exercise of His greatest skill. Thus Southwell concluded the process, begun in the Roman novitiate 10 years earlier, of abandoning every right to power of choice over his own body and soul: he contemplates giving his body over to the executioner to prepare it for the art of God. It is hardly surprising that in the later passages of the book a tone of insouciance appears in the presence of even the most unimaginable kinds of torment:

> One death, is no more death than another, and as well the easiest, as the hardest, taketh our life from us. Which point a glorious Martyr of our days executed for the Catholic Faith in Wales, having well understood, when the sentence of his condemnation was read that he should be drawn upon a hurdle to the place of execution, then hanged till he were half dead, afterward unbowelled, his head cut off, his body quartered, his quarters boiled, and set up in such and such places, he turned unto the people, and with a smiling countenance said, and all this is but one death. (123b)

From the government's point of view, *An Epistle of Comfort* can only have appeared to be an extremely dangerous book, its author an equally dangerous man. A reader who took it seriously would be set free of every kind of secular allegiance in the service of a pure idea. Death, the ultimate sanction of state power, would have no terror in it; in fact the more terrifying and violent the death, the better for the martyr's purpose. As the government was to discover in its own dealings with Robert Southwell, such commitment to the art of martyrdom not only rendered the normal instruments of power useless: it forced the government to participate in a pageant enacting its own illegitimacy and impotence. Southwell's *Epistle* is the literary counterpart to his own martyrdom, transforming horror into beauty, disgrace into honor, and defeat into victory:

> Let our adversaries therefore load us with the infamous titles of traitors, and rebels, as the *Arians* did in the persecution of the *Vandals*, and as the *Ethnics* were wont to call Christians *Sarmentitios, et semiasios*, because they were tied to halfpenny stakes, and burnt with shrubs: So let them draw us upon hurdles, hang us, unbowel us alive, mangle us, boil us, and set our quarters upon their gates, to be meat for the birds of the air, as they use to handle rebels: we will answer them as the Christians of former persecutions have done. *Hic est habitus victoriae nostrae, hec palmata vestis, tali curru triumphamus, merito itaque victis non placemus.* Such is the manner of our victory, such our conquerous garment, in such chariots do we triumph. What marvel therefore if our vanquished enemies mislike us. (133a)

Finally, one's thoughts return to Philip Arundel, Southwell's martyr-designate, reading his director's instructions in the Tower of London. In 1589 he was brought to trial on the charge of treason before his peers in the House of Lords. He was found guilty and sentenced to the usual horrible death. The sentence was extremely unpopular, and the government never carried it out. Arundel, of course, could not know about that in advance, and as he waited for death Robert Southwell wrote to him again. It is a long letter, and there is no word in it of sorrow, regret or sympathy, no mention of the wife and children he would never see again. Instead, it is a curious combination of congratulation and exhortation. The earl is a fortunate man; he knows the time, the manner, and the place of his death; he knows the cause in which he dies, and the reward that awaits him. The martyr's death not only brings its own crown, but absolves him of all sin. Of course, human beings are frail creatures and do not always recognize their own good: "Let therefore neither fury nor fiction nor the sword, nor glory of splendid attire, nor bribes, nor entreaties, nor any other violence seduce thee from the charity of Christ." The letter then ends with some practical advice, that the earl should not afflict himself too much with fasting, prayers, and penitential works, "in order that [he] may be the stronger for the last combat," and the author signs off: "I desire you the happiest issue of the conflict begun. Let us hope by the help of God to see each other hereafter in glory. Farewell."[8]

In solitary confinement, under sentence of death, totally isolated from the ordinary flow of human life and contact, Philip Arundel is the embodiment of Southwellian man, his comfort a sheet of paper consigning him to the absolute as rigorously in its own way as his judges' sentence. He died in the Tower in 1595, apparently of natural causes (though some thought he was poisoned) not long after Southwell himself was executed.

Mary Magdalen's Funeral Tears: Origins

In every way the *Funeral Tears*[9] is a different kind of work from the *Epistle.* Herbert Thurston, one of the first writers to attempt criticism of Southwell, thought that it was an example of John Lyly's Euphuism, a "curiously affected style . . . in favour in Italy, Spain, and France," and in keeping with "the somewhat perverted literary taste of that period." He believed that admirers of Southwell's "perfect earnestness and simplicity" would find his use of so affected a style puzzling, and suggested that the style was a disguise analogous to the actual disguises used by priests in England, as well as a means to an end: familiarity with current literary fashion was a "passport to the good graces of casual fellow-travellers."[10] Janelle, while agreeing that the style of the *Funeral Tears* is often precious and sentimental, pointed out that although there are some Lylyan touches in the book, in general the tone and style are unlike

Lyly and owe more to Southwell's familiarity with patristic writing. "When compared to his contemporaries of the Euphuistic school, Southwell appears to us as remarkably modern. He has got rid of the many-limbed unwieldiness of Lyly's prose, of its uncouth lumber and gaudy stage properties. He has discovered good taste" (Janelle, 194). Nonetheless, Janelle thought that *Funeral Tears* was Southwell's first prose work, and he attributes the change from its preciosity to the "manliness" (198) of the *Epistle* to the author's developing experience and maturity.

Janelle based his opinion upon the fact that what look like two preliminary drafts of the *Funeral Tears* survive at Stonyhurst College in a little manuscript collection of autograph materials dating from Southwell's Roman days. Janelle also knew that these drafts were translations of a homily on Mary Magdalen that also survives at Stonyhurst in an Italian version ascribed to St. Bonaventura; but because one of Southwell's versions begins, "In this present solemnity having to speak in this audience of your charities we are put in mind that Mary," he thought Southwell meant to preach his text as a sermon on some feast day (Janelle, 184–85). Christopher Devlin then added to these hypotheses by claiming to know the occasion for which Southwell preached his sermon. A government spy reported that on 22 July 1586, the feast of St. Mary Magdalen, a priest preached a sermon on the subject of Mary in the Marshalsea Prison to an audience including the daughters of Sir John Arundell; since *Funeral Tears* is dedicated to Dorothy Arundell, the priest must have been Southwell (Devlin, 117–18). Unfortunately for this theory, Southwell's letter of 25 July to Aquaviva makes it clear that on 22 July he was still with Father Weston at a house in the country, looking forward to solemn mass sung to William Byrd's music (Pollen 1908, 308; Devlin, 114).

Helen White brought order to this confusion when she pointed out that Southwell's drafts were translations of a popular medieval homily usually ascribed to Origen, published in Latin in England early in the sixteenth century (probably in 1504) and again in English in 1565.[11] The sentence that Janelle interpreted as Southwell's prelude to a sermon is in some, though not all, versions of the original homily. Although, as White argues, it would be very difficult to rule out the possibility that Southwell consulted the Italian version, there can be no doubt that Southwell's translation was based on the Latin original because—a fact not known to White—phrases from it are written between the lines of his text (Nancy Brown, not knowing that these are phrases from the original, treats them as evidence of Southwell's difficulties with English: "At a loss for suitable words or synonyms in English, Southwell has written Latin equivalents between the lines" [*Poems,* xxi]). Furthermore, detailed comparison of the English translation of the homily with *Funeral Tears* shows that before Southwell finished work on his book, he even used his English predecessor's work as well as the Latin original.[12]

Although Southwell began work on the subject of Mary Magdalen in Rome, there is no evidence that he finished it there, or that he finished it much before its publication in 1591. Similarly, in the case of the *Epistle,* although there can be little doubt that he completed the book in England, it is very likely (even though no manuscript evidence survives) that he began work on so congenial a theme before he left Rome. Janelle's theory that Southwell's prose style matured between the writing of *Funeral Tears* and the *Epistle* has no basis in the evidence, and cannot explain the difference between the two works. Southwell was not a writer who lived out his own development in his work. His gift was at the service of his order and the Church, and the difference between these two books' styles is owing first to their subject matter, and second to the fact that the *Epistle* is written for a man, the *Funeral Tears* for a woman.

Southwell sent both books into the world as professionally as he could, and it is a further sign of his stylistic adroitness that he adopts so easily the manner of the fashionable dedicatory epistle or address to the reader. As in the *Epistle,* so in *Funeral Tears* there is an address to the reader deploying the conventional topos of the reluctant author: "Yet sith the copies thereof flew so fast, and so false abroad, that it seemed in danger to come corrupted to the print: it seemed a less evil to let it fly to common view in the native plume, and with the own wings, than disguised in a coat of a bastard feather . . ." (sig. A8). If this were really true, it is peculiar that no manuscript copy has survived to be treasured by some Catholic owner. More interestingly, he presents his book as a challenge to current taste, adopting a satirical tone as he does so. "And sure it is a thing greatly to be lamented, that men of so high conceit [he means contemporary writers of prose fiction] should so much abase their abilities, that when they have racked them to the uttermost endeavor, all the praise that they reap of their employment, consisteth in this, that they have wisely told a foolish tale, and carried a long lie very smoothly to the end" (sig. A7–7v). His book, in contrast, is based on scriptural truth, his method and style imitate the patristic writers, and its purpose is to teach the reader "to love without improof of purity." Moreover—a touch that must have given intense pleasure to Southwell and his friends—the book was licensed for printing by the archbishop of Canterbury himself, and in due course printed by a regular London printer, Gabriel Cawood, who may himself have had Catholic sympathies (Devlin, 234).

Mary Magdalen's Funeral Tears: The Book

Mary Magdalen had always been a very popular saint: aristocratic, penitent, and very beautiful. As a fair penitent she had a particular appeal for the Counter-Reformation world: "The remorse felt for the moral perversion of the Renaissance period accounts for the tearfulness in fashion after the Council of Trent, which inspired Valvasone's poems, *Le lagrime della Maddalena*" (Janelle, 189). As a student in Rome, Southwell was familiar with the fashionable literature of remorse and tears, which inspired his own *Funeral Tears* and *Saint Peter's Complaint.* His epistle dedicating the *Funeral Tears* to Mistress D. A. leaves no doubt that, like his Italian contemporaries, he wished to divert current literary taste from profane and secular to religious subject matter.

"Mistress D. A." was Dorothy Arundell, daughter of Sir John Arundell of Lanherne, Cornwall, a wealthy west country aristocrat (Janelle, 59). According to Southwell, she had asked him for a book about Mary Magdalen. In response, he gave a her a book about Mary's funeral tears, not treated as tears of penitence but, rather surprisingly, as tears expressing "the great vehemency of her love to Christ" (sig. A3), a theme chosen because, as he says, the age is a passionate one, and love is its dominant passion.[13] That being so, nothing could be more important than "to draw this flood of affections into the right channel." Then follows the famous sentence: "Passions I allow, and loves I approve, only I would wish that men would alter their object and better their intent" (sig. A3v). Once again, therefore, as in the *Epistle,* Southwell is writing about a theme of his own formation as a Jesuit, in this case the redirection of the passions, and especially love, from an earthly to a heavenly object. In fact, the *Funeral Tears* is really a story, cast in the form of a homiletic meditation, about a woman's overwhelming love for an infinite object, "such a love as could never exceed, because the thing loved is of infinite perfection"; should anyone ask Father Southwell about his qualifications to write such a story, he has a disarmingly simple, candid reply: "I know that none can express a passion that he feeleth not, neither doth the pen deliver but what it copieth out of the mind" (sig. A6). In Dorothy Arundell's case, Southwell's understanding of love and his alteration of its object may have been successful; she died a Benedictine nun at Brussels.

The gospel narrative of Mary Magdalen's coming to Christ's tomb on Easter morning (John 20.1–18) is the basis of both the *Funeral Tears* and of the homily from which it is derived. The homily, which grows to a work about three times its original length in Southwell's hands, provided the outline and some of the contents of Southwell's book. Both works are meditations on Mary's experience, cast in the form of a dialogue between Mary and the other persons present—the angels in the empty tomb, Christ himself, and the narrator—but Southwell's tone is quite different from the homilist's, owing to the detail, intensity, range, and polish of his writing. To see how radically Southwell altered his original, one can compare his version of Mary's mistaking Christ for a gardener with the original. First, the homilist's version: "Thou supposest him to be a gardener, to shew thou knowest him not. For Jesus is also a gardener, because he soweth all good seed in the garden of the soul, and in the hearts of his faithful he planteth every good herb." Southwell's version is entirely different. He develops a long typological harmony between the garden of the tomb, the garden of Gethsemani, and the garden of Eden, and between Christ and Adam as gardeners:

> For as our first father, in the state of grace and innocency, was placed in the garden of pleasure, and the first office allotted to him, was to be a gardener: so the first man that ever was in glory, appeareth first in a garden, and presenteth himself in a gardener's likeness, that the beginnings of glory, might resemble the entrance of innocency and grace. And as a gardener was the foil of mankind, the parent of sin, and author of death: so is this gardener, the raiser of our ruins, the ransom of our offenses, and the restorer of life. (sig. G6)

He concludes the passage (which is four times as long as the passage quoted) by saying that Mary was permitted to make her mistake so that "we might be informed of the mystery, and see how aptly the course of our redemption did answer the process of our condemnation." Patternmaking of this kind, both in the content and in the prose that expresses it, explains much of the appeal of the *Funeral Tears.* It is a clever, charming work, despite the initially discouraging fact that Southwell has expanded a gospel narrative of 18 verses into a 25,000-word book.

The book's two most striking literary qualities, its emotional power and its vividly realized scenes, reflect Southwell's professional training as a Jesuit in the arts of meditation and self-examination, often in quite tiny details. His two angels, for instance, are stately, dignified creatures, "as swift as thy thought," who make no movement at all until Jesus appears. Then, as Mary is answering their question, "Why weepest thou?" she sees the angels "with a kind of reverence rise, as though they had done honor to one behind her," whereupon, as in the gospel narrative, she turns and sees Jesus, without recognizing him. Southwell has visualized the scene as accurately as if he were dramatizing it and changed it in the process. The gospel's Mary simply "turned herself back," perhaps only to leave the tomb in disappointment; Southwell's Mary turns because of the angels' movement. He can be extremely realistic, too. In her grief at finding the tomb empty except for the grave clothes, Mary assumes that "some malicious pharisee or bloody scribe" has stolen the body. Her passionate speech of complaint, however, does not impress the narrator. "O Mary," he asks her, "why dost thou thus torment thyself with these tragical surmises?" and proceeds to show her that the evidence does not support her conclusion. What thief would have stolen the body and left the grave clothes neatly folded? Even more to the point: "When thy master was stripped at the cross, thou knowest that his only garment being congealed to his gory back, came not off without many parts of his skin, and doubtless would have torn off many more, if it had been anointed with myrrh: Look then into the sheet, whether there remain any parcel of skin, or any one hair of his head: and sith there is none to be found, believe some better issue of thy master's absence, than thy fear suggesteth" (sig. D6–D8v).

Did Southwell owe this remarkable passage of detective work to the habit of contemplating the passion during the third week of the *Spiritual Exercises,* and particularly to the famous "mental representation of the place," the visualizing of the persons present, and the consideration of Christ's sufferings in his human nature?[14] Southwell's presentation of sacred persons and events as real people of flesh and blood and as concrete realities with all their physical detail is a feature of the art and literature of the baroque age often attributed to the influence of Ignatius and his exercises. Whether Ignatius was the determining influence or whether he was himself a manifestation of a tendency of the period is a hard question to decide.

Some of the book's most powerful moments seem to reflect the Ignatian method of focusing the emotions on the subject of meditation by means of a colloquy, either with one of the persons of scripture or even with oneself. Mary's agonized cry of longing to suffer with her beloved Jesus is such a moment, carrying the reader into the heart of the

Counter-Reformation's affective devotion: "I would be nailed to the same cross, with the same nails, and in the same place: my heart should be wounded with his spear, my head with his thorns, my body with his whips: Finally I would taste all his torments, and tread all his embrued and bloody steps" (sig. C8v). Later, when Jesus himself appears, and Mary fails to recognize him through her tears, the narrator himself produces a similar colloquy when Jesus asks her, "O woman why weepest thou, whom seekest thou?" "O desire of heart, and only joy of her soul," the narrator asks, "why demandest thou why she weepeth, or for whom she seeketh?" There is, of course, an answer, which the narrator eventually provides; Mary has been seeking the living among the dead. Yet the narrator's initial response, which is a protest from the heart on her behalf at such an apparently cruel question, draws one's attention to the real nature of this book, which has been obscured for successive readers because of the mistaken notion that because Southwell based it upon a homily, he intended it for a sermon. It is nothing of the kind.

As Southwell tells it, the narrative of Mary's visit to the tomb in the first hours of Easter day is a moving love story about a woman who has lost the man who means more to her than anything in the world to a very cruel, agonizing death. Early in the morning, as soon as the prohibited time of the Sabbath is past, she goes to anoint his body in the tomb, and finds it gone. Then, as she stands in sorrow, having just told the angels, "They have taken away my Lord, and I know not where they have put him," she turns to find, against every hope, that he has come back to her alive. Southwell's method of telling the story is to visualize the scene and the actors clearly, and to track its development through every detail of his heroine's feelings. As he explained in "To the Reader," the difference between his story and his competitors' is that his is true; therefore, like the homilist, he has included the gospel narrative in his text, where it provides the stages or stations of its unfolding. Nonetheless, the real story is Mary's story.

All Mary's thoughts and actions proceed from her love, as all-encompassing as its object is infinite: "He was the total of her loves, the height of her hopes, and the uttermost of her fears" (sig. B4v). As Southwell presents her, she is a heroic woman, far braver than Peter and John, who come with her to the tomb, but who leave her alone there because they are "fearful of farther seeking" (sig. B4v). Later, when she mistakes Jesus for the gardener, and asks him whether he has moved the body, and if so to tell her where it is, Southwell devotes a long passage to the absolute courage of the promise contained in her words, "I will take him away."

At that moment, such is the power of love that Mary, who has already come to the tomb before daylight prepared to roll away the stone despite the guard, has no fear of authority, no fear of the mutilated corpse, and no fear of her own capacity to carry it: "Love is not ruled with reason, but with love. It neither regardeth what can be, nor what shall be done, but only what itself desireth to do. No difficulty can stay it, no impossibility appall it" (sig. H4–H4v).

The central episode of the book, to which everything leads and from which the climax develops, is the touching moment when Jesus appears. Impressively developed as the first part is, the conclusion leading to the revelation of Jesus and the reversal of Mary's grief probably has no equal for sustained emotional and intellectual power in Elizabethan prose. It begins with the famous apostrophe to Mary's tears, "But fear not, Mary, thy tears will obtain," which is a prose hymn on tears as a sacrament of penitence, compassion, and mercy, able to remake the cosmos:

> They tie the tongues of all accusers, and soften the rigor of the severest Judge. Yea they win the invincible, and bind the omnipotent. When they seem most pitiful, they have greatest power, and being most forsaken they are most victorious. Repentant eyes are the Cellars of Angels, and penitent tears their sweetest wines, which the savor of life perfumeth, the taste of grace sweeteneth, and the purest colors of returning innocency highly beautifieth. This dew of devotion never falleth, but the sun of justice draweth it up, and upon what face soever it droppeth, it maketh it amiable in Gods eye. (sig. H7v–H8)

Southwell's critics and biographers, motivated by admiration for his life and animated by hagiographical zeal, have consistently misunderstood his approach to style—as demonstrated in a passage like this—interpreting its mannered artifice either as a concession to the taste of his time or as a way station on the road to the kind of plain style thought suitable for saints. The truth is, as Brian Oxley has pointed out, "that Southwell's sense of the artifice of holy things, and indeed, of the holiness of artifice, is central to his life and work."[15] The apostrophe to Mary's tears makes it very clear that the inhabitants of Southwell's heaven are delighted connoisseurs of the human performance at its best: "No no, the Angels must still bathe themselves in the pure stream of thy eyes, and thy face shall still be set with this liquid pearl." Moreover, as this sentence shows, the almost infallible rhythm of Southwell's prose can correspond, in a reader's mind, with an answering gracefulness of line and gesture in the figures he is imagining. The result is an aesthetics of holiness, a literary equivalent to the visual splendors of Counter-Reformation baroque art and architecture. Janelle's notion (116ff.) that Southwell's education under Jesuit masters disciplined and cramped his imagination into the frigidity of artifice and conceit is the reverse of the truth. It is far more likely that Southwell's aestheticism was encouraged by his education, and especially by his use of Ignatian meditation. As any reader can discover by experiment, the "mental representation of the place" is not only difficult; it inevitably leads to an art of selection, arrangement, and display upon the internal stage of the mind; and that is the stage upon which the action of the *Funeral Tears* takes place.

The book's greatest challenge to its author came in the last ten pages, when Jesus finally comes back to Mary, reveals himself by speaking her name, and then immediately seems to withdraw with the strange words, "Do not touch me." First, Mary's tears of sorrow turn to tears of happiness, and except for the one word, "Master," she is unable to speak: "For such is their estate that are sick with a surfeit of sudden joy, for the attaining of a thing vehemently desired" (sig. I3). Then, "to supply the want of words with more significant actions," she falls at his feet (as she had done once before when she anointed his feet with precious ointment [John 12.3]), and "offered to bathe them with tears of joy, and to sanctify her lips with kissing his once grievous, but now most glorious wounds" (sig. I4). As the antithesis of "grievous" and "glorious" in that sentence hints, Southwell is conscious of an impending and impassable gulf of contradiction to be negotiated, between heaven and earth, between the glorified and the merely human body, between, in short, different worlds. Why, he asks, if a sinful Mary was able to kiss Christ's mortal feet, is a Mary "alive in grace" forbidden to kiss the glorious feet of the body that has returned for her salvation?

Southwell gives the answer to Jesus himself. Mary must now learn the difference between a glorious and a mortal body, and she must prepare herself for the final loss of His ascension to His father: "It is now necessary to wean thee from the comfort of my external presence, that thou mayest learn to lodge me in the secrets of thy heart, and teach thy thoughts to supply the offices of outward senses. For in this visible shape I am not here long to be seen, being shortly to ascend unto my Father: but what thy eye then seeth not, thy heart shall feel, and my silent parley will find audience in thy inward ear" (sig. I6v). In the presence of those exquisitely cadenced words, Mary begins the process of change, not without intense regret and sorrow, from a disciple, friend, and lover into a type of the modern Christian woman, who can only know the divine persons in the recesses of her own heart. The book then ends with a short homily to the reader: "O Christian soul, take Mary for thy mirror, follow her affection that like effects may follow thine. . . ."

Mary Magdalen's Funeral Tears inhabits a wide range of human experience from the very ordinary to a zone verging on the mystical. This is the effect of Southwell's intention: to take ordinary experience and channel it towards the divine. There is nothing abstract about his thesis that a knowledge of divine love is rooted in the experience of human love. Southwell reveals a surprising knowledge of love, both in his treatment of Mary ("Her thoughts were arrested by every thread of Christ's Sindon" [sig. B6v]), and in the many apt aphorisms about love and the behavior of lovers that he sprinkles through the book, for example: "In true lovers every part is an eye, and every thought a look" (sig. C4); "But maugre all fears, love's hopes will work to the highest pitch, and maugre all hopes, love's fears will stoop to the lowest downcome" (sig. C6v); "For when things dearly affected are lost, love's nature is never to be weary of searching even the oftenest searched corners, being more willing to think that all the senses are mistaken, then to yield that hope should quail" (sig. B6).

There is also a suggestion of an allegorical tendency to be found in the work, which is already present in the source, but which Southwell developed according to his own preoccupations. Allegorically speaking, Mary stands for the Christian soul, separated by violence from the living Christian truth that is her only happiness. More specifically, she is an English Catholic woman, and the violence that threatens her is that of contemporary England, just as the voices that cajole her to abandon her weeping have their parallel among those in England who were tempting the Catholics with the rewards of compromise and apostasy.

The book was extremely popular and much imitated, going through 10 editions by 1636 (McDonald, 109–11). Most of the imitations give the impression of opportunism. Nicholas Breton's *Marie Magdalen's Love* (1595), a sermon on John 20.1–18, is a straight theft from Southwell, meant, like the *Funeral Tears,* for a female audience. It is mixed in genre, being partly a meditation in imitation of Southwell, partly a sermon in the common Protestant manner, "dividing" the text and applying it figuratively to the listener or reader. It would be a mistake to imagine that Breton, a literary jack-of-all-trades, had undergone some kind of conversion. The same is true of Thomas Nashe, whose *Christ's Tears over*

Jerusalem was mocked by Gabriel Harvey: "Now he hath a little mused upon the *Funeral Tears of Mary Magdalen,* and is egged on to try the suppleness of his Pathetical vein" (Devlin, 266).

Thomas Lodge, who became Catholic and married a waiting woman to the Countess of Arundel, presents a somewhat different case. His *Prosopopeia. The Teares of the Holy, Blessed, and Sanctified Marie, the Mother of God* (1596), dedicated to the countesses of Derby and Cumberland, mentions Southwell's work, and is his response, "cleansed from the leprosy of my lewd lines,"[16] to Southwell's challenge to write on moral and religious themes. The book is a prose meditation spoken mostly in the voice of Mary after the Crucifixion as she, Joseph, Mary Magdalen, and others prepare Christ's body for the tomb. Lodge catches Southwell's tone in his opening passages, but cannot sustain it for long. He draws on Bernard and patristic writings, so that one finds phrases such as "thou flaming bush . . . thou flourishing rod . . . thou lock of Gideon," but his natural style is a variety of Euphuism, distinguished by an elaborate syntax and much allegorizing from nature.

> The Naturalists write, that Bats have weak sight, because the humor Crystalline, which is necessary for the eye to see with, is translated into the substance of the wings to fly with, whereupon they have leathern wings, and so for their flight sake, have lost their sight, because that is subtracted from the eyes, which is employed in the wings. These bats betoken these proud neglecters, who by how much the more they strive to fly, by so much more are they deprived of the grace of the divine light, because all their intention, which ought to be in consideration of heavenly things, is translated into the feathers of ambition, so that all their thought is how they may ascend by degrees the steps of dignity, not descend in imitation of thee, to the bosom of humility. (sig. E1v.–E2)

Much of Mary's speech is in this pedantic style, and consequently the work, like Breton's, is a hybrid. Lodge has not understood Southwell's disciplined focus on the psychology of Mary Magdalen at a particular moment, and he lacks Southwell's instinct for form as well as his ear for prose rhythms. As is so often the case with truly original works of art, the real nature of the *Funeral Tears* escaped its imitators.

An Epistle of Robert Southwell unto His Father

This letter,[17] in which Southwell asks—or rather instructs—his father to return to the Church, first appeared in print in 1596–97 in the first edition of *A Short Rule of Good Life,* printed secretly in England by Henry Garnet on his second printing press. It also made its way, along an independent line of transmission from the original, into the three major manuscripts of Southwell's collection of lyric poems (*Letters,* xlviii–l). It seems likely, therefore, that it was circulating in manuscript before it was printed, and that that avenue of publication opened during the author's life. It may even have been as much a public as a private document from the start. It is not written in the style of a familiar letter. As Janelle observes (149), it is "decidedly rhetorical," a formal composition. Although the letter is dated 22 October 1589, Brown suspects that there is a copyist's error in the year, and that the letter may have been written in 1587, or even 1586; if this were so, one would expect a variant date to appear somewhere among the manuscript copies.

At the time of the letter, Southwell's father, Richard, was in financial difficulties. The family's house at Horsham St. Faith, Robert's birthplace, was sold in 1588 to Sir Henry Hobart. In 1589 Richard was in prison for debt, and his son Richard, Robert's elder brother, was under instructions from the Privy Council to pay his brother Thomas's very large debts (*Letters,* xxiii). There is a suggestion in Southwell's letter that his father had been a bad businessman. The family's financial problems, however, seem to have originated in the previous generation, with old Sir Richard Southwell's peculiar marital arrangements. This man, Robert's grandfather, had married an heiress, Thomasine Darcy, but had produced children by her cousin, Mary Darcy, whom he married off to one of his own servingmen. When Thomasine died, he convicted the servingman of bigamy, and took Mary as his second wife, and had one last, legitimate child by her. All the older children were illegitimate, a situation that caused serious and very expensive trouble with blackmail and litigation in the next generation (Devlin, 8). In any case, as head of the family, Southwell's father had failed to preserve his estate, and therefore the family itself; he had married again, and fallen, in his son's phrase, "into the puddle of schism" (*Letters,* 20) by attending Church of England services: "You have long sowed in a field of flint which could bring you nothing forth but a crop of cares and affliction of spirit, rewarding your labors with remorse, and affording for your gain eternal damages . . . Though you suffered the bud to be blasted and the flower to fade, though you permitted the fruit to be perished and the leaves to dry up, yea, though you let the boughs wither and the body of your tree grow to decay, yet, alas, keep life in the root for fear lest the whole become fuel for hell-fire" (8, 10).

Seen against a background of family disunity and ill-feeling, Southwell's letter to his father is a curious document, touched by tones of anger, even of contempt, not found in his other writing. Southwell claimed, in his letter to Sir Robert Cecil, as in his *Spiritual Exercises,* to have returned to England to be a pastor to his family (*Letters,* 81; *Exercises,* 93), but it is clear from the opening paragraphs of the letter to his father that he was not welcome to many of his kinsfolk: "Yet, because I might very easily perceive by apparent conjectures that many were more willing to hear of me than from me, and readier to praise than to use my endeavors, I have hitherto bridled my desire to see them with the care and jealousy of their safety, and banishing myself from the scene of my cradle, in my own country I have lived like a foreigner, finding among strangers that which in my nearest blood I presumed not to seek" (*Letters,* 4).

It would have been very dangerous for his relations to welcome him into their houses. At the same time, it is also apparent from the closing passages of the letter that Southwell had spoken with at least some of his brothers and sisters, who agreed with him in disapproving of his father's second marriage and change of religion: "I have expressed not only mine own but the earnest desire of your other children, whose humble wishes are here written with my pen; for it is a general sore that sitteth at all our hearts . . . to see our dearest father, to whom both nature hath bound and your merits fastened our affections, to be dismembered from the body to which we are united" (19).

As Nancy Pollard Brown says (xx), Southwell's method of argument is to "unsettle his protagonist," and the striking expression "dismembered from the body" is both an example of the method and of a willingness to be ruthless, even cruel in speech. The metaphor has a double ground. The first is the famous passage on the body of Christ (1 Corinthians 12.13–27): "For the body also is not one member, but many . . . And if one member suffer anything, all the members suffer with it; or if one member glory, all the members rejoice with it." The second ground of the metaphor is the peculiarly literal significance of "dismembered from the body" as a part of the punishment for treason, enacting the victim's separation from the communal body of the nation. The son who daily expects to be literally dismembered from the body of the state is in effect telling his father that he is in the far worse condition of being metaphorically dismembered from the body of Christ. One can take the measure of the violence of Southwell's expression by comparing it to a similar metaphor in Shakespeare's *I Henry IV,* 4.1.42–43:

WORCESTER: Your father's sickness is a maim to us.
HOTSPUR: A perilous gash, a very limb lopp'd off.

Worcester's "maim" carries the suggestion of the loss of an arm or leg, and the thought is repeated in Hotspur's "limb lopp'd off," but in both expressions the idea is softened to the thought of a severe wound, or even of a branch cut from a tree. Whereas Shakespeare's mind recoils from the image of dismemberment, Southwell's insists upon its literal horror as a figure of his father's spiritual condition.

In this letter, too, for the first time, the careful art of Southwell's prose can be self-protective, even self-disguising, containing or concealing personal motives and feelings within the antitheses of a polished, authoritative irony; for example, "I was loath to enforce an unwelcome courtesy upon any, or by seeming officious to become offensive" (3). Under the law, Southwell's office rendered him publicly offensive to the government and many of the people of England; officiousness was inseparable from his position, because he was a priest by office, endowed in his own eyes with supernatural authority. "I exhort you, therefore, as the vice-gerent of God," he writes, "and I humbly request you as a dutiful child, that you would surrender your assent, and yield your soul to God's merciful inspirations" (19); he thus drives home the paradoxical consequences of his rank with that ambiguous phrase "dutiful child," applicable both to himself and to his father, but almost certainly intended, with a kind of angry paradoxicality, for his father. That officious sentence might well appear offensive to a recipient. Rationally and intellectually, Southwell probably understood the difficulty, even the falseness, of his position. He spends four long paragraphs justifying his assumption of superiority over his father, even ending with a little joke about his childhood nickname, "Father Robert." Yet his two cogent examples of scriptural young people called by God to right wrongs, David and Daniel (5), act in circumstances of profound social disorder, and their youth itself, read with the typologizing eye of a Robert Southwell, could only be a sign of reversal and social upheaval in the world they were called to act in.

It may be that Southwell interpreted the divisions in his unhappy family as typical or representative of the ills of England, and if so, that may explain why pious Catholics copied the letter with so much admiration. Intent upon the typical they did not see the particular, and lost the son in the priest and the father in the apostate. Although it is possible to interpret the letter as an example of the higher priestly authority calling the lesser paternal authority home to its true allegiance and duty, one can only do so by omitting the personal element in it from one's reading. Admit that, and it becomes apparent that in this case, the higher authority is empowering filial emotions of anger, disappointment, and even shame.

Most twentieth-century readers' minds will shrink from the contemplation of a son preaching hell-fire to his father, trying to frighten him into Catholicism by dwelling upon his failures and his approaching death, and never, throughout a long letter, ever expressing any but the most formal respect for him, let alone love, sympathy, or admiration. Few will agree with Devlin's summing up: "There is no note of scolding in the letter; it is a masterly mingling of the stern warnings of a priest, 'God's vice-gerent', with the loving loyalty of a younger son" (202).

Power—both the need to exercise it and to submit to it—is one of the unargued themes of Southwell's prose, itself an exercise of power in literary form designed to win souls for his Church. The unargued axiom, the authority of the church itself, is always taken for granted. Perhaps Southwell's father was, as his son implies, a poor businessman who took life insufficiently seriously and who disappointed his children by marrying again; but the argument from personal failure has little to do with Southwell's conclusion, as surprising as it is violent: "He cannot have God for his father that refuseth the Catholic Church for his mother" (18). There is a splendid absurdity about such statements that leads one to suspect that the man who makes them is not so much thinking as avoiding thought; he is substituting syntactical and rhetorical aesthetics for thought, and this, it has to be confessed, is a frequent tactic of Southwell's prose, as in the concluding sentence of the letter: "Howsoever, therefore, the soft gales of your morning pleasures lulled you in slumbering fits, howsoever the violent heats of noon might awake affections, yet now in the cool and calm of the evening retire to a Christian rest and close up the day of your life with a clear sunset, that leaving all darkness behind you and carrying in your conscience the light of grace, you may escape the horror of an eternal night and pass from a mortal day to an everlasting morrow" (*Letters,* 20). Reading this son's exhortation to his father might remind one of Shakespeare's portrait of a son, Hamlet, bullying his mother with a mouth full of metaphors and a head too full of clichés to admit any real idea of what her life might actually have been like. Stripped of its conventional metaphor, Southwell's peroration simply means that since his father's life is virtually over, he has nothing to lose and everything to gain by being reconciled to the Church. The persuasion is in the metaphor. Life is a day, and death is its sunset; how much nicer to follow the sun into the west than to die in the darkened east. Not for the first time in Southwell's prose, the metaphor is more vividly realized than the reality it represents.

One unintended consequence of Southwell's often quite outrageous exercises of power in his writings is that one becomes very conscious of, and sympathetic to, his recipients. One's heart aches for Philip Arundel, receiving *The Epistle of Comfort* in the Tower 400 years ago. Even in the case of Dorothy Arundell and the *Funeral Tears,* one feels there should have been someone to warn her that she was reading a very beautiful, very powerful, but dangerously persuasive book. In the *Epistle of Robert Southwell unto his Father,* Richard Southwell emerges as a more sympathetic figure than his son. Not many fathers, in addition to an undistinguished life, financial difficulties, and family squabbles, have to undergo the further trial of having a Jesuit son telling him, in a publicly circulated document, to acknowledge his failures, repent for his sins, and become a Catholic. Nonetheless, in that world of types, analogies, and correspondences, our sympathy would probably be rejected. Philip Arundel died a martyr, Dorothy Arundell died a nun, and Richard Southwell, said Henry Garnet, died a Catholic (Devlin, 203).

Chapter Three

Southwell's Prose: The Second Stage

The Triumphs over Death

The three works considered in this chapter, *The Triumphs over Death, A Short Rule of Good Life,* and *An Humble Supplication to Her Majesty,* all date from late 1591, when Southwell had been in England more than five years. Since the style and tone of Southwell's prose varies with the subject and the recipient, one cannot really talk confidently of a development in his prose style. Nonetheless, there is a difference of tone between these last works and their predecessors. There is a purely literary exuberance in the prose of the first pieces that Southwell owed to the luxury of inexperience. It is one thing to contemplate martyrdom in a mood of imaginative enthusiasm, another thing entirely to live with the daily threat of capture, torture, and death. Writing about hell-fire and the advisability of a good death to an aging man one has not seen for 12 or 13 years is not at all the same thing as sitting with people, and watching the play of feeling in their eyes as one talks. Southwell's last three pieces show the effect of five years' experience. Each of them is about real-world events and actions, and though in each Southwell's favorite themes and images recur, the tone is sober, practical, and subdued.

The first, *The Triumphs over Death,* came into existence because of a death in the Howard family. Philip Howard, Earl of Arundel, was the son of his father's second wife, Lady Mary Fitzalan. He had a half-sister, Margaret Howard, who was the daughter of his father's first wife, Margaret Audley. Lady Margaret Howard married Robert Sackville, the son of Thomas Sackville, Earl of Dorset, author of *Gorboduc* and of the Induction to *The Mirror for Magistrates.* In August 1591, Lady Margaret died at age 29, and Southwell wrote a consolatory epistle for her brother.

The publication of this little work in 1595 under the title *The Triumphs over Death* sheds a little much-needed light upon the circulation, publication, and audience of Southwell's works. Like the *Epistle of Robert Southwell to his Father, The Triumphs over Death* circulated in both manuscript and printed form. Its text, like that of the *Epistle,* appears in three of the major manuscripts of Southwell's lyric poems, the Stonyhurst or Waldegrave Manuscript (Stonyhurst MS A.v.27), the Virtue and Cahill Manuscript (now deposited at the Bodleian Library), and British Library Additional Manuscript 10422. None of these manuscripts can be certainly dated, but the best of them, the Stonyhurst Manuscript, was written before 1608 or 1609 on paper made in the 1580s (*Poems,* xxxvii–viii). Although Nancy Pollard Brown believes that the collection of poems in these manuscripts was based upon a prior collection prepared by an associate of Southwell's at the time of his arrest (xxxv–vi), she does not hazard an opinion about their prose contents. Nonetheless, it seems likely that the manuscript circulation of both the poetry and the prose dates from the author's own lifetime. There is evidence for this proposition in Southwell's own prefatory statement to the reader of *Triumphs:* "I intended this comfort to him whom a lamented fortune hath left most comfortless; by him to his friends, that have equal portions in this sorrow. But I think the philosopher's rule will be here verified, that it shall be last in execution, that was first designed, and he last enjoy the effect, that was first mover of the cause."[1] This evidently means that Southwell, having originally written the work for Arundel to read and then send to others, was unable to send it to him because of his close imprisonment, and so distributed it himself to its secondary audience.

Consequently, we find once again that Southwell has written a work for a specific recipient, but with the intention of distributing it to a larger audience. In this case, moreover, the larger audience received it before the recipient. The publication of *Triumphs* in a quarto edition in 1595 complicates the question of the audience even further, and raises the intriguing probability that the combination of prose and poetry in the manuscripts originated with Southwell himself.

A minor poet called John Trussell edited the little 1595 quarto. Almost nothing certain is known about him, although some probabilities coalesce about his name. He was the author of at least two poems: a translation of Thomas Watson's *Amintae gaudia,* published in 1594 under the title *An Old Fashioned Love,* and another imitative poem, *The First Rape of Fair Helen,* published in 1595 and related to a Latin poem by Watson on the rape of Helen that was published in 1586. In 1595, according to a poem by an anonymous "T. T." prefixed to *The First Rape of Fair Helen,* Trussell was very young; "T. T." even calls him a boy. Only one perfect copy of *The First Rape of Fair Helen* survives. When A. W. Rosenbach of Philadelphia bought this book, he believed he was buying a very rare work with Shakespearean connections. The report of the sale in *The Times Literary Supplement,* 9 July 1931, prints a prefatory sonnet from the book (which Rosenbach thought might be addressed to Shakespeare), and includes an account of the Trussells, a Stratford family associated with both the Ardens and the Shakespeares. Dr. Rosenbach also suggested a link between the poet Trussell and a historian of the same name, mentioned in the *Dictionary of National Biography,* who lived in Winchester. A week later, S. C. Wilson wrote to the *TLS* (16 July 1931) to say that John Semple Smart had shown that Thomas Trussell of Billingsley, a manor in Stratford, had been involved in Thomas Arden of Wilmcote's purchase of the Snitterfield estate that came to Shakespeare's father through his wife, Mary Arden.[2] In fact, William Shakespeare and the Trussells of Billingsley were probably related. The question is whether John Trussell the poet was a member of that family or not.

The Trussells had held Billingsley since the reign of Henry II. In the sixteenth century, they suffered the common misfortune of losing an heir, so that an infant inherited. This was Avery Trussell, who succeeded his grandfather in 1517. He was put in ward, and during the wardship the estate was stripped and little Avery was married to the spoiler's daughter. It seems that the Trussells never recovered from this misfortune. Avery's son John succeeded him, and he in turn was succeeded by Thomas, a soldier. On 6 August 1585, Thomas committed a robbery and was attainted and condemned to death in 1588. Whether the sentence was ever carried out is unclear. The estate passed to the Crown, and with its sale to Sir Robert Lee in 1600, the long residence of Trussells in Stratford came to an end.[3]

In 1934, Mark Eccles announced that he would discuss the identity of John Trussell, but unfortunately he never did this.[4] Stratford records of the period produce no John Trussell of an age suitable for the poet. An early seventeenth-century visitation of Hampshire, however, attributes a son named John to Henry Trussell, the brother of John Trussell of Billingsley, and this son of Henry would be about the right age for the poet (*Pedigrees,* 223). As M. A. Shaaber discovered, however, visitations contradict each other, and the birth and parentage of John Trussell the poet remain elusive.[5]

This is a pity, because the literary connections implied are interesting. Shaaber produces evidence from the text of *The Rape of Fair Helen* that Trussell had read Shakespeare's *Rape of Lucrece* (417). Moreover, there are five close verbal parallels between Trussell's "To the Reader" and Shakespeare's dedications to *Venus and Adonis* and *Rape of Lucrece.* Shaaber attributes them to coincidence, but five parallels between such short texts seem too many for coincidence.[6] If Trussell were related to Shakespeare, and sufficiently interested in his books to imitate them, then we have a hint of a literary and social milieu in which works were discussed and circulated, and in which Trussell's editing of *The Triumphs over Death* in the same year that he published *The Rape of Fair Helen* is as much the work of a young man keen to make himself known in literary circles as it is a gesture by a Catholic partisan—not that literature and Catholicism are mutually exclusive enthusiasms. Trussell was undoubtedly Catholic; it is a question of the balance of interests in his approach.

Unfortunately, the possibilities are difficult to judge objectively precisely because the figure of William Shakespeare is hovering in the background of the question. The implication that Shakespeare was moving in, or even admired in, Catholic circles seems to have been the reason for M. A. Shaaber's rather defensive approach to the question of Trussell's identity and allegiances. Yet Christopher Devlin presents a good case for Southwell's influence on *Rape of Lucrece* (269–73), which was composed before Southwell's poems were available in print and when they were circulating only in manuscript. John Trussell's role in the publication of Southwell's work indicates the existence of at least one channel through which Shakespeare and other interested writers could have had access to Southwell's writing. Thomas Watson, Marlowe's raffish friend, whose *Amintae gaudia* Trussell translated, had been resident intermittently at the English College in Douai from 1576 to 1577. He was there in the summer of 1576 and left in October, returning in May 1577 to leave again in August. His stay at the college thus overlapped with the young Southwell's, whom he would have known. His first work, a Latin translation of *Antigone* (1581), was dedicated to the Earl of Arundel. Arundel was not Catholic at the time, and there is no reason to believe that Watson was Catholic; but Watson evidently knew people in Catholic circles familiar with Southwell, and before his death in late 1592 could have been a conduit for distributing Southwell manuscripts among other writers. Like Southwell, Watson had lived in Italy and brought Italian influences back to England with him (Eccles, 131–44).

Trussell dedicated *Triumphs* to Lady Margaret's four children. In his dedicatory poem he explained that the author had made his own arrangements for the work's publication, but that his death had "orphaned" it. Trussell, therefore, is the work's "foster-sire," and he has dedicated "this fruit of Southwell's quill" to the four young people because the lady commemorated in it is their mother and because

Southwell originally wrote it for their uncle. Shaaber suggests that Trussell was the children's tutor, "or employed in some other household capacity" (Shaaber, 413), but a dedication to the subject's children would have been a natural one in any circumstances. Interestingly enough, the same publisher, Busby, issued the volume of Southwell's poems called *Moeoniae,* which he entered in the Stationers' Register on 17 October 1595 just a month earlier than *Triumphs.* In his address to "the Gentleman Readers" Busby says that unless the poems live in his readers' memories, they will otherwise "die in an obscure sacrifice." Trussell uses a similar expression in his dedicatory poem about *Triumphs,* "the which till now clouded, obscure did lurk" (*Triumphs,* xi). If the verbal similarity, joined to the closeness in date of publication, is a sign that one author wrote the dedicatory matter for both volumes, then Trussell spoke truly when he said he was a "foster-sire," that is, a literary executor who was responsible for the publication of both *Triumphs* and *Moeoniae.* Even the rather learned Latin title, *Moeoniae* (more correctly *Maeoniae*)—meaning "of, or pertaining to Maeonia or Lydia," associated with Homer and lyric poetry—hints at Trussell's editorship, since he was evidently a very good Latinist. Speculation of this kind is necessarily tentative; nonetheless, if Trussell were the editor of both books, then in the light of what we know about the manuscript tradition, it is virtually certain that he owned the poetry and the prose in a single manuscript, which, as he seems to suggest, Southwell prepared.[7]

In addition to the dedicatory poem in *Triumphs,* Trussell provided two more. A contemporary reader encountering all three poems for the first time will have been surprised, perhaps even startled, to see Southwell's name spelled out in full in each of them. Even though the authorship of *Saint Peter's Complaint* must have been an open secret in 1595, neither Southwell's name nor initials appear on the title page. His initials only are on the title page of *Moeoniae.* Trussell, however, seems to have been determined to blazon Southwell's name upon his edition of *Triumphs.* The second poem is an acrostic on ROBERT SOUTHEWELL, spelling the name out in the margin and using it in the text. The third poem, which recommends the work to all readers of good taste, includes a cheerful attack on "our late sprung sectaries," and "Bible-bearing hypocrites" who, "To read what *Southwell* writ will not endure," because of their knowledge of the author's religion. Southwell's name, therefore, appears four times in three short poems.

Trussell's most subtle declaration of his own faith and of his homage to Southwell appears in the third poem, "To the Reader," in the form of an invitation to the readers to share his interpretation of the work before them. In the manuscripts, presumably including Trussell's own manuscript, *Triumphs* has no title, and so it is very likely that *The Triumphs over Death,* a phrase Trussell uses in the poem, is Trussell's title. It is significant that in the title *Triumphs* is plural, for when the phrase appears in the poem, the word is singular:

> I thought it best the same in public wise
> In Print to publish, that impartial eyes
> Might, reading judge, and judging, praise the wight
> The which this Triumph over Death did write. (*Triumphs,* xiii)

Could anyone read those lines in London in 1595 and not reflect that Southwell had enacted as well as written a triumph over death? The next stanza explains how a work originally written for and about one person came to be for and about many, including its readers:

> And though the same he did at first compose
> For one's peculiar consolation,
> Yet will it be commodious unto those,
> Which for some friend's loss, prove their own self-foes:
> And by extremity of exclamation,
> And their continuate lamentation
> Seem to forget, that they at length must tread
> The self same path which they did that are dead.

The important question is, who are they that were dead in late 1595? Of the people connected directly with the writing of this epistle, there is Lady Margaret herself, then Robert Southwell the author, and thirdly the recipient: Philip Arundel. Addressed in the piece as if he were already almost a dead man, he died in the Tower in August 1595. Finally, the invitation to the readers, both those who have suffered loss and those who have not, to accept the author and his work, widens immensely the circle of those concerned in its meaning. Only "our late sprung sectaries," whom "no perswades suffice," exclude themselves from the circle by their dislike of Southwell and his works.[8] Thus the triumphs implied by Trussell's presentation are multiple, and his plural title makes sense.

In sum, Trussell encourages us to read the piece in more than one way. First, he asks us to read it as a piece addressed to the Earl of Arundel concerning his sister's death. Second, he wants us to enjoy it as evidence of the quality of the mind and work of "Our second Ciceronian, *Southwell.*" Third, we are to read it in the context of the deaths of both author and recipient, and, fourth, in the context of our own life and impending death. An epistle written for the earl thus becomes Southwell's premonitory statement on his own death as well as on all those other deaths.

To what extent, one wonders, did Southwell intend this widened field of reference? What did it mean in the fall of 1591 to console and advise a man living under a sentence of death for the loss of a favorite sister? What did it mean to write such a book when at any moment one might be captured, tortured, and executed oneself? Since landing in 1586, Southwell had survived five years in England, but by February 1592 Garnet was writing to his superiors in Italy, "There is simply nowhere left to hide" (Devlin, 274). Janelle, reading the book with apparently no sense of its context, finds it a puzzling work, a curious mixture of stoicism, practicality, and Christian resignation. There is certainly a strong vein of stoicism in it; it could even be described as a Senecan epistle. (As Christopher Devlin noticed, Southwell evidently knew Seneca's epistle to Marcia, consoling her for the death of her son.) Not to feel sorrow, Southwell tells the earl, is brutish, but to mourn immoderately is effeminate: "This impotent softness fitteth not sober minds. We must not make a life's profession of a seven nights' duty, nor under color of kindness be unnatural to ourselves" (*Triumphs,* 3). Death is common to all, he writes, and "Nature did promise us a weeping life" (15). The earl, moreover, is a nobleman, and has an example to set: "Nobility is an aim for lower degrees to level at marks of higher perfection, and like stately windows in the worthiest rooms of a politic and civil building, to let in such light, and lie open to such prospects, as may afford their inferiors, both means to find and motives to follow heroical virtues. If you should determine to dwell ever in sorrow, it were a wrong to your wisdom, and countermanded by your quality" (17–18).

Underlying these characteristically Senecan passages recommending a tight-lipped, stoical reserve is the encouragement to be true to oneself. Its most startling expression appears towards the end of the work in an image of the mourner as a soldier who, his comrade having been shot at his side, wastes no time in feeling sorry for him but rescues himself:

> If we will think of her death, let it be as of a warning to provide us, sith that which happeneth to one, may happen to any, yea none can escape that is common to all. It may be the blow that hit her, was meant to some of us, and this missing was but a proof to take better aim in the

> next stroke. If we were diligent in thinking of our own, we should have little leisure to bewail others' deaths. When the soldier in skirmish seeth his next fellow slain, he thinketh it more time to look to himself, than to stand mourning a helpless mischance, knowing that the hand that sped so near a neighbor cannot be far from his own head. But we in this behalf are much like the silly birds, that seeing one stick in the lime-bush, crying to get away, with a kind of native pity are drawn to go to it, and so mesh themselves in the same misfortune. (28–29)

"This strangely dry-hearted and scarcely uplifting spiritual selfishness," as Janelle describes it (236), seems to him quite uncharacteristic of Southwell and unchristian in spirit. He thought its cause lay in a doomed attempt to combine a repellent classical stoicism, "harsh, aloof, and scarcely human," with Christian resignation based upon acceptance of original sin and trust in God.

The first and most obvious comment to make about these passages in *Triumphs* is that Southwell did not write them in a country vicarage with the scent of hollyhocks blowing through the window and the Sunday roast in the oven. He wrote them in conditions of terrible danger, both to him and to his friend. The soldier who loses his comrade is an image of Southwell himself, watching fellow priests being captured and killed. The stoicism of *Triumphs* is the mood of a man who, like a World War II fighter pilot, has to fly until he is killed himself. For the first time, we hear Southwell speaking as an aristocratic, classically educated humanist to a fellow aristocrat in the words of the great, ancient commonplaces about death: "This general tide washeth all passengers to the same shore, some sooner, some later, but all at the last" (*Triumphs,* 13), and his purpose is to clear the mind of useless, distracting emotion: "If sorrow cannot be shunned, let it be taken in time of need, sith otherwise being both troublesome and fruitless, it is a double misery and an open folly" (15). The second point is that Southwell's stoicism is meant to be severely practical advice on maintaining presence of mind and a sense of proportion before impending death. Imitate the merchant, he advises, who lost wife, children, and fortune in one shipwreck: he visited a lazar hospital, "where finding in a little room many examples of greater misery, he made the smart of others' sores a lenitive to his own wound" (30)—a passage that carries one into the moral world of *King Lear* and Edgar's announcement of a rock-bottom principle on which one might decide to continue living in the face of horrors: "The worst is not / So long as we can say 'This is the worst'" (4.278–28). *Triumphs* is not, as Janelle seemed to think, a rhetorical exercise in the combination of classical and

Christian modes. There is indeed a combination of modes, but it seems to be the fruit of experience, not of theory, as when Southwell tells the earl, "I am loth to rub the scar of a deeper wound for fear of reviving a dead discomfort; yet if you will favor your own remedies, the mastery over that grief that sprang from the root, may learn you to qualify this that buddeth from the branch" (19).

The Christian corollary to Southwell's classical stoicism is faith in the peace and joy of another life infinitely more precious than this earthly one, to which earthly life is a prelude and for which humanity was created. So, summing up a graceful evocation of Lady Margaret's life and character, Southwell returns to a favorite image of God as artist and gardener and writes, "Let him with good leave gather the grape of his own vine, and pluck the fruit of his own planting, and think so curious works ever surest in the artificer's hand, who is likeliest to love them, and best able to preserve them" (10). Moreover, we belong in the artificer's house, and in dying Lady Margaret has followed her children home who had died before her: "She sent her first fruits before her, as pledges of her own coming, and now may we say that the sparrow hath found a home, and the turtle dove a nest, where she may lay her younglings" (19).[9]

The passage most tenderly expressive of the relationship between brother and sister, the one newly dead, the other on the threshold of death, takes this image of moving back home in its most homely form, and links it in a harmony of images evoking a return to one's true place:

> The more you tendered her, the more temperate should be your grief, sith seeing you upon going, she did but step before you into the next world, to which she thought you to belong more than to this, which hath already given you the last ungrateful congé. They that are upon remove, send their furniture before them; and you still standing upon your departure, what ornament could you rather wish in your future abode, than this that did ever so highly please you? God thither sendeth your adamants whither he would draw your heart, and casteth your anchors where your thoughts should lie at road; that seeing your loves taken out of the world, and your hopes disanchored from this stormy shore, you might settle your desires where God seemeth to require them. (21)

With its plain language, gracefully managed syntax, and strong, slow-moving rhythm, this prose is as disciplined as the frame of mind it recommends. Only towards the very end of *Triumphs* does Southwell permit himself some of the emotional intensity of his more elaborately figurative style, as he draws his reader to contemplate God as the center and destination of life in this world: "Let God strip you to the skin, yea to the soul, so he stay with you himself. . . . Think him enough in this world that must be all your possession for a whole eternity" (31). The last evocation of Lady Margaret herself in that new life blends a note of almost ecstatic anticipation with a sudden and surprising homeliness: "She stood upon too low a ground to take view of her Savior's most desired countenance, and forsaking the earth with good Zaccheus, she climbed up into the tree of life, there to give her soul a full repast of his beauties" (33).

Janelle preferred the *Epistle of Comfort* because "It breathed an exhilarating enthusiasm in the glad acceptance of tribulation," whereas *Triumphs,* despite the "concinnity" of its prose ("as melodiously balanced and as free from visible tricks of repetition as ever"), is disappointingly sober and rational (236–38).[10] The answer is surely that the *Epistle* was in many ways a presumptuous, even naive book, for all its brilliance and power; *Triumphs* was the fruit of five years' experience of death's real presence. One should also add that even so carefully crafted an epistle as *Triumphs* has its nugget of news to impart to its readers. It leaves them in no doubt that Lady Margaret made a good death, that she died a Catholic, and that there were Catholics in attendance at her death. In 1591, that was important news.

A Short Rule of Good Life

According to Henry More, Southwell wrote this little "how-to" book[11] for the Countess of Arundel; its exact date is not known. When Henry Garnet came to publish *Short Rule,* probably sometime between 1596 and 1597, he wrote in his preface that "amongst the last of his fruitful labors for the good of souls," Southwell had himself intended to publish the book, a statement that dates the book with *Triumphs* and the *Supplication.* Once again, too, one notices that although Southwell wrote with a particular recipient in mind, he intended publication for a larger audience.[12]

Strictly speaking, *Short Rule* is not a literary work at all. It is a practical manual of a kind that became very popular in the sixteenth century, instructing pious lay Christians in the art of living a Christian life. Such manuals reflect the most dramatic change of the period in European Christianity, by which a church dominated by monastic Christianity became one organized more and more for worship by lay people. In Protestant countries such as England, the monasteries were simply abolished, and the laity, in effect, took over almost complete control of the church. In Catholic countries the effects of the same change were felt, even though the religious orders were not abolished. The aims of the Counter-Reformation demanded for their realization a clergy that was out in the world, teaching, preaching, and converting the laity. Of the new orders, the Jesuits were the very embodiment of the new spirit. For instance, in Robert Persons's blueprint for a reformed English Catholic Church, members of religious orders were expected to support themselves by active practical work. Persons's scheme also shows why reconciliation between Protestant and Catholic remained impossible. Although Persons was prepared, even eager, to redirect the Church's resources to the service of the laity, he was not prepared to cede any of the clergy's authority to them. Indeed, as John Bossy observes, Persons's financial proposals "implied something like a social counter-revolution, a redistribution of wealth and power back from the gentry to the clergy" (22–23).

Views of this kind would naturally be reflected in the practical manuals. In England, the Church's first attempt to satisfy lay demand for devotional material produced the pious anthologies called the Primers, published first in Latin, later in English. A Primer would include, among other things, a calendar, various prayers (on leaving the house, for instance, or taking holy water), the hours of the Virgin and similar devotions, and the penitential psalms. They are charming books, but much of the material in them was decidedly secondary to a fundamental knowledge of Christianity, and such instruction as they included was really based on monastic practice. Some Primers included an essay, "The manner to live well, devoutly and salutarily every day," translated by Robert Copland from the French of Jean Quentin (*Letters,* xxxi), but its recommendation to assign such activities as meditation, prayer, examination of conscience, and reading the office to set times of day was not really very practical for a layperson. On the other hand, the Church was determined not to put primary materials, in particular the Bible, into lay hands at all.

The genius of Ignatius Loyola resolved the contradiction of aims between Church and laity when he invented his *Spiritual Exercises.* He took the difficult, highly specialized, professional subject of ascetic and contemplative theology and rationalized it into a set of sequential exercises that anyone could perform. The exercises were meant in the first place for the training of his Jesuits in disciplined obedience to God and the Church, but Ignatius also meant them to be useful to other interested people. Very soon Jesuit spiritual directors were giving the exercises to laymen, and clergy of other orders, especially the Dominicans and

Franciscans, were adapting the Ignatian approach to devotional manuals for the laity. The work of the Spanish Dominican Luis de Granada became especially popular in England. In Jesuit hands, however, the exercises, given to the laity in retreats, solved perfectly the problem of satisfying the laity's wishes for a more developed understanding of the religious life while maintaining clerical authority. In fact, the Ignatian exercises passed on to the laity the Jesuit principle of obedience to the superior in the form of complete obedience to the confessor or spiritual guide.

Southwell's *Short Rule* is a book conceived on Jesuit principles. It begins, like his own *Spiritual Exercises,* with the laying of foundations for a good life; in this case there are five of them, which define the reader's relationship to God and the principles of life that follow upon it. These foundations place one in a dramatic and challenging situation. First, one is created, preserved, and redeemed to serve God in this world, and enjoy Him in the next. From this it follows that we are His, body and soul, and bound to serve Him more than any other creature in the world. Second, our salvation is our most important business, to which everything else should be subordinate. Third, if we serve God in this world, and prepare to enjoy Him in the next, we must be prepared for every kind of hindrance from the world, the flesh, and the devil. Fourth, the weapon of these enemies is sin, which "maketh our souls more ugly than the plague, the leprosy, or any other most filthy disease doth the body" (*Letters,* 25). Fifth, since we are God's creatures, made to serve Him, we are tenants only in this life and must be ready to present an account of our stewardship to our landlord. Southwell then lays down the fundamentals of our relationship to God in seven "affections" towards Him: love, fear, zeal for His honor, continual praise of Him, an intention to serve Him in every action, perfect resignation of oneself to Him, and gratitude.

Having founded his reader's relationship to God upon self-denial and abnegation, Southwell then turns to the human relationships, to superiors, to neighbors, and to oneself. The chapter on superiors is mostly about a spiritual superior and the obedience owed to him:

> First, I must procure to love him as a parent or father, by which name such men in the Church of God are called, endeavoring to carry myself towards him as dutifully (not only in spiritual things but also in those temporal wherein I might justly fear any sin) as a well-nurtured child behaveth himself towards his natural father . . . Secondly, I must reverence and honor him as the vicegerent of God, and consider Christ in his person, and do my duty to him as if in him I did see Christ . . . Thirdly, I

> must avoid such things as may cause in me any unjust discontentments or dislike towards him . . . Fourthly, to obey him in all things wherein I see not any express sin, taking his words when he counseleth, commandeth, or forbiddeth me anything as the words of Christ, agreeable to the saying of our Saviour: "He that heareth you, heareth me, and he that despiseth you, despiseth me." (*Letters,* 33–34)

Curiously enough, duty to one's neighbor is confined entirely to social matters, and the instructions upon deportment can be summed up in the phrase, "Be a gentleman!" One is to be dignified and cheerful, and keep one's emotions in the range of "Modest and temperate affection" (35). Talk and laughter are to be seemly and modest, clothing to be handsome and clean, "and as much as may be, without singularity: "To conclude, the virtues necessary in conversation are modesty, decency, affability, meekness, civility, and courtesy, show of compassion to others' miseries and of joy at their welfare, and of readiness to pleasure all and unwillingness to displease any" (36–37).

Chapter 5, "Of my Duty towards Myself," conveys the same air of reason and moderation. One must lead an orderly, planned life, keeping "due times of rising, meals, and going to bed," and having decided upon an order, one must keep to it: "I must not flit from one exercise to another, from one ghostly father to another, from one form of behavior to another" (39). Gentlemanly urbanity does not have the last word, however: "As I must take heed of pampering my body too much and ought to take some ordinary corporal punishment of fasting, discipline, haircloth, or the like, so on the other side I must have care of my health, and temper all my spiritual exercises and bodily afflictions with discretion" (40). The remainder of the book gives detailed instructions for the arrangement of one's day, the supervision of servants and children, behavior in sickness, and concludes with extended passages on coping with temptation and on "Considerations to Settle the Mind in the Course of Virtue."

As these selections show, *Short Rule* is in many ways a courtesy book. Southwell wrote it for wealthy readers with households to run, business to attend to, and social responsibilities to meet. His social advice on running a household, bringing up children, looking after servants, and spending time wisely probably reflects his own tastes and upbringing; it also places him in the company of contemporaries like the Calvinist William Perkins. *Short Rule,* like Perkins's *Government of the Tongue,* is a founding document of English social and domestic life in the modern world, inculcating the standards of decency, moderation, and, above all, respectability that used to be taken for granted in most upper- and middle-class households. It was a popular book, being printed eight times in the 60 years after Southwell's death (Janelle, 252), and it is not surprising that, like Robert Persons's *Book of Resolution, Short Rule* circulated in versions edited for Protestant use.

Southwell's householder is a dignified, cheerful, and urbane man of the world. He runs a genial establishment, treats his servants kindly but firmly, but brings up his children rather severely. He keeps a pleasant table, at which he suits his conversation to the company, being sure "to direct mine attention to talk either for dispatch of necessary business, if there be any, or for maintaining mutual love and charity, if it be merry or ordinary talk" (36). He sounds more like a figure from the eighteenth than the sixteenth century, and he seems to be a different person from the submissive penitent who treats his confessor's instructions as the word of God, and who, in the privacy of his own room wears a hair shirt and flagellates himself.

In *Triumphs* Southwell's ardor for sacrifice found itself tempered by the reality of death and suffering among decent, charming, lovable, and, above all, innocent people of his own kind and class. In this little book, the whole well-learned ecclesiastical structure of submission and mortification encounters the facts and realities of the social lives of the people he was writing for. The Catholic gentry were no more ready than their Protestant brethren to submit to clerical supervision. "Members of the lay aristocracy," writes John Bossy, "who claimed the right to live as Catholics, did not do so because they hankered after the *status ante quo,* still less after the revived clericalism of the continental counter-Reformation": "Titles to church property, repugnance to prelatical government, moved them as deeply as anyone else, and they came to see how decisively their status was enhanced where plurality of religion became a way of life. All in all, they were better off controlling the destinies of a minority sect in a country dominated by their Protestant counterparts, than playing second fiddle in a uniform society of the Catholic clergy's devising. Upon this rock nobody was going to build a church" (32). The hair shirt and the whip hardly belong in the houses of people like that.

Short Rule is a pastoral book, and in it Southwell has tried, with his customary clarity and elegance, to link the interests of his people and of his superiors. The division in the book between sacred and secular priorities may be owing to the possibility that, as Janelle thought, it was never really finished. There are passages of great eloquence in the sections devoted to ascetic theology:

> He that entereth into the way of life must remember that he is not come to a play, pastime, or pleasure, but to a continual rough battle and fight against most implacable and spiteful enemies. And let him resolve himself never in this world to look for quiet and peace, no, not so much as for any truce for a time, but arm himself for a perpetual combat . . . Let him see and peruse the pattern of his Captain's course, who from his birth to his death was in a restless battle, persecuted in his swaddling clouts by Herod, annoyed the rest of his infancy by banishment, wandering, and need; in the flower of his age slandered, hated, pursued, whipped, crucified, and most barbarously misused. (61)

Nonetheless, this writing belongs to a different world from the sections on social advice, where there is little suggestion at all of "continual rough battle." Garnet's claim in his preface that *Short Rule* would prepare its readers for martyrdom cannot be based on disinterested criticism. The unknown redactor of the Folger manuscript assessed the book more accurately when, with very few changes, he turned it into an Anglican document. The dissonance in Southwell's book is testimony to his own truth as a writer, hinting at a prophecy uttered as if by instinct of the failure of the triumphalist mission to England and of the marginalizing of the clergy's call for lay submission.

An Humble Supplication to Her Majesty

The problem of power in Southwell's prose comes into sharper focus, if not to a definite resolution, in his masterpiece, *An Humble Supplication,* written in December 1591. In October 1591 a proclamation drawn up, under the queen's name, declaring "great troubles pretended against the realm by a number of seminary priests and Jesuits, sent, and very secretly dispersed in the same, to work great treasons under a false pretence of religion." The occasion for the proclamation was the landing of a Spanish force in Normandy, which the proclamation interpreted as part of a stratagem for invading England concocted by the king of Spain and his "*Milanois* vassal," the pope. The role of the priests and Jesuits in such an invasion was to spread disaffection among the people. As political commentary, those were at least debatable propositions, but in other respects the proclamation was an affront to any decent standard of discourse. It described the priests as "a multitude of dissolute young men, who have partly for lack of living, partly for crimes committed, become fugitives, rebels, and traitors." In Rome and Spain and other places, the proclamation claimed, they gathered in "certain receptacles" to be instructed in "school points of sedition" before being smuggled into England, where they hoped, after a Spanish invasion, to be enriched with their fellow-subjects' property. Moreover, it added, such people and their supporters in England were punished under the laws against such treasons "and not for any points of religion," as they liked to claim. After all, "a number of men of wealth in our realm professing contrary religion are known not to be impeached for the same, either in their lives, lands, or goods, or in their liberties, but only by payment of a pecuniary sum as a penalty for the time they do refuse to come to church." After an attack on the characters of Robert Persons and Cardinal Allen, described as "seditious heads, being unnatural subjects of our kingdom (but yet very base of birth)," the proclamation then provided instructions for improving security, but without moderating its vituperative tone: "They do come into the [realm] by secret creeks, and landing places, disguised, both in their names and persons. Some in apparel, as soldiers, mariners, or merchants . . . And so generally all, or the most part, as soon as they are crept in, are clothed like gentlemen in apparel, and many as gallants, yea in all colors, and with feathers, and such like disguising themselves, and many of them in their behavior as ruffians, far off to be thought, or suspected to be friars, priests, Jesuits, or Popish scholars."[13]

The peculiarity of the proclamation, as Geoffrey Hill pointed out, was that it mingled downright lies and insult with "well-timed cynical gestures of mock reasonableness and tolerance." The claim that recusants were not impeached for religion except for "payment of a pecuniary sum," writes Hill, considered on its own terms, "without reference to executions and incarcerations," is "the most wilful and monstrous cant," and "far more numbing than the most savage vituperation" (Hill, 24). The Catholic writers living in exile responded quickly with pamphlets as violent and insulting in their way as the proclamation itself, which only provoked the government further (*Supplication,* x–xi). At home in England, among those actually affected by the proclamation, Southwell, no doubt after consultation with Garnet, prepared an entirely different kind of response, working very rapidly. The proclamation seems to have been issued in late November, and Southwell's reply was finished by the end of December (*Supplication,* 11).

Quite apart from any distress Southwell felt over the proclamation's lies about his own priestly function, he interpreted its harassment of the already helpless and miserable Catholics as a misuse of the royal power, one liable moreover, because of its gross language, to bring the Crown into disrepute at home and abroad. In the England of Elizabeth, a subject suffering hardship under the misuse of power or from the applications of the law could, in theory at least, seek redress by direct petition to the Crown, on the legal principle that the Crown itself could do no wrong, and that as part of its prerogative it embodied a general principle of justice under the name of equity. Equity in principle and procedure, again in theory at least, was the basis of the prerogative courts, of Star Chamber, of Ecclesiastical High Commission, and of Chancery. In practice, however, Robert Southwell no more had access to the Crown's equity through its courts than by direct petition,[14] and so he did the only thing he could do, which was to transform a petition on grounds of equity into a literary address to the Crown—a courageous and momentous step.

He began with an address to the queen. "Most mighty and most merciful, most feared and best beloved Princess," he wrote, and proceeded to assume that the queen herself was not responsible for the proclamation, which could only be the work of people who had arrogated the royal power to themselves for their own purposes. He assumed further that the queen must be ignorant of the true character of her Catholic subjects and of the conditions under which they were living. Southwell's queen, therefore, to whom he addressed his *Supplication,* was not so much the historical Elizabeth Tudor as she was that mysterious entity the Queen of England, embodying in her sacred person the realm and its people, its deepest, most enduring character, and its best hopes for its future condition. Southwell wrote as the subject of that realm to its ruler and embodiment, and the essential theme of his book is that the realm has lost itself in lies, violence, and lawlessness. He had said something similar in 1588 when he wrote to Aquaviva a letter describing the appalling violence against the Catholics in the wake of the Spanish Armada. He began that letter by saying that he was reluctant to describe events in England because he feared that the behavior of the persecutors "should bring more hatred on the English name than the constancy of our Martyrs would win for it praise," and he ended by begging Aquaviva not to judge his country by its violence: "Your Paternity should regard the situation in this light. The constancy of the Catholics is such as is always admired in a people naturally inclined to piety, but the fury and cruelty of the enemy is not to be regarded as a disgrace on the nation, but as the outcome of the pestilent heresy, which does violence not only to religion, but to the laws and restraints of nature" (Pollen 1908, 325, 328).

Southwell's assumptions about the separateness of the queen from the realm had momentous consequences for his understanding of the present state of his country and for his prose. Southwell's England is a place where, as in Shakespeare's histories, appearances and realities have diverged, and truth is hidden. Southwell's perception that truth is now hidden produces its most dramatic effect in a long section of the *Supplication* devoted to an explanation of the Babington Plot against Elizabeth as a "sting" operation, "to draw into the net such green wits as . . . might easily be overwrought by Master Secretary's subtle and sifting wit" (*Supplication,* 18).[15] Southwell's primary intention in this passage was to clear Catholics in general of any complicity in the plot, and to argue that Babington and his associates, whatever else they were, were Secretary Walsingham's dupes as well. In the course of making his case, Southwell mentions several characters in Walsingham's employment who, in encouraging others to act treasonably, must have acted treasonably themselves, and yet were never prosecuted for it. The further implication is that Master Secretary Walsingham himself acted treasonably in the same way, both by inciting others to treason, and by using the authority and credit of the Crown to further the aims of his own faction. In other words, in Southwell's version of the Babington Plot, elements of the government were themselves guilty of treason. A Shakespearean parallel to the historical moment revealed by Southwell appears in *King John,* 4.3.142–47, when the Bastard, Falconbridge, decodes for the audience the visual image of Hubert with the body of Prince Arthur, the rightful heir to the throne, in his arms:

> How easy dost thou take all England up!
> From forth this morsel of dead royalty
> The life, the right and truth of all this realm
> Is fled to heaven; and England now is left
> To tug and scamble, and to part by th'teeth
> The unow'd interest of proud-swelling state.

In the play and in the *Supplication,* the realm, emptied of life, right, and truth by illegitimate government, is no longer itself, its royalty hidden or lost, and subverted.[16] Similarly, the queen whom Southwell addresses no longer inhabits the proscribed and buried England for which he speaks. As he tells her, if the "day of general resurrection" were to happen in her time, millions of returning prelates, pastors, and religious people would be "amazed to see their relics burned, their memories defaced." The queen's "predecessors and fathers, with the peers and people of the realm" would be equally amazed to find themselves made felons under her laws, "for erecting bishoprics, endowing churches, founding colleges . . . yea and for giving their ghostly fathers in way of relief but a cup of cold water, though it were at the very point of death" (29–30).

Southwell's conviction that in England truth is hidden and must be brought to light animates the whole of the *Supplication.* As R. C. Bald noticed (*Supplication,* xvii), in answering the proclamation Southwell used the standard controversial method of the period, which was to refute his opponent "phrase by phrase and section by section." Nonetheless, despite this intrinsically dull method, "the *Supplication* possesses continuity and unity in an unusual degree" (*Supplication,* xvii). The reason for this is not only that the book "is animated by the orator's passion," as Bald puts it, but that in every point he makes, Southwell is exposing the same kind of untruth that aroused his passions in the first place. Detail by detail, he accumulates his picture of a realm separated from its own truth, religious, political, and social, and in so doing he becomes the spokesman, not just for the Catholics and their priests, but for the whole realm, tainted and violated by the government's behavior:

> We verily presume, that none of your Majesty's honorable Council would either show so little acquaintance with the prince's style, as to deliver in your name, a discourse so full farced with contumelious terms, as better suited a clamorous tongue than your highness' pen; or be so slightly affected to the regard of your honor, as to defile it with the touch of so many false assertions . . . And though the injury offered to your Majesty, and nearly concerning all your realm, might in equity challenge all men's pens to warn you of so perilous courses: yet sith priests and Catholics are the marks chiefly shot at; we ask humbly leave of your Majesty and Council, to shew, how choleric the humor was towards us, that cared not though the arrow hit your Majesty's honor in the way, so the head thereof might enter into our hearts. (*Supplication,* 2)

As Geoffrey Hill insists, the term "in equity" is crucial in the shaping of Southwell's argument and the making of his prose. Equity in practice is redress, balance, satisfaction. "In equity," as Southwell writes, an injury as universal as that inflicted by the proclamation challenges a universal response, even if only one man steps forward to make it. In the courts of equity, clamor, contumely, and rage must encounter reason, quiet, and gentleness; the lie must be exposed to the truth. Like Piers Plowman, who "put forth his head," or like G. K. Chesterton writing, "For we are the people of England, that never have spoken yet,"[17] Southwell puts himself forward, impelled by the necessity of the moment to speak for the unheard people. His prose, a plain periodic style, measured, cadenced, balanced, and shorn of any but the most vigorously functional figures of speech, is the perfect medium for his purpose. It can refute the proclamation's sillier lies with urbane contempt, as when it responds to the accusation that the Catholic priests are of "base birth": "This only we may say in answer of our objected *baseness;* that in the small number of the Catholic priests of our nation (which reacheth not to the tenth of the Protestant ministry) there are very near as many, yea happily more gentleman, than in all the other clergy of the whole realm" (*Supplication,* 7). In rebutting the accusation that the priests have come over to be enriched by a Spanish invasion, it can rise to a kind of tragic wittiness: "For to say we do it upon hope to be enriched with those possessions that others now enjoy hath but very small semblance of probability, considering how much likelier we are to inherit your racks and possess your places of execution, than to survive the present incumbents of spiritual livings, or live to see any dignities at the king of Spain's disposition" (14). And it rises effortlessly above the vulgarities that pass for analysis in the proclamation:

> Yet it hath been objected sometimes against priests, that they should pretend to kill your sacred person, a thing so contrary to their calling, so far from their thoughts, so void from all policy, that whosoever will afford reason her right, cannot with reason think them so foolish to wish, much less to work such a thing, every way so odious, no way beneficial. We come to shed our own, not to seek the effusion of others' blood. The weapons of our warfare are spiritual, not offensive. We carry our desires so high lifted above so savage purposes, that we rather hope to make our own martyrdoms our steps to a glorious eternity, than others' deaths our purchase of eternal dishonor. (32)

The climax and focus of the *Supplication,* however, is in the concluding pages indicting the government of savage cruelty in its treatment of prisoners and Catholics, rich and poor. There can be no doubt that in Southwell's description of Elizabethan methods of torture and imprisonment we read the results not only of information received and digested, but of his contemplative mastery of his own certain fate. "Mental representation of the place," the imagining of the place one is meditating upon, recommended in the Jesuits' *Spiritual Exercises,* is a phrase sometimes lightly used in literary criticism with little sense of what it really entails. Southwell's account of Elizabeth's jails is a mental representation of many places, and all of them are uninhabitable to most imaginations:

"Divers have been thrown into unsavory and dark dungeons, and brought so near starving, that some for famine have licked the very moisture off the walls. . . . Some with instruments have been rolled up together like a ball, and so crushed, that the blood sprouted out at divers parts of their bodies" (34). What distinguishes Southwell from virtually all his contemporaries in these contemplations of horror is that he shows no sign of interest or pleasure in the subject; there is no hint of an emotional or writerly collusion with the torturers and persecutors. The entire passage is an indictment made out of compassion and humanity. The same is true of the succeeding pages on the sufferings of the Catholic laity, "made the common theme of every railing declaimer; abused without means or hope of remedy, by every wretch, with most infamous names" (40). Here Southwell takes on the big lie upon which all the other, smaller lies of the proclamation were founded, namely, that "We suffer nothing for religion." On the contrary, he writes, we suffer everything for religion, and nothing else but religion; and once again he is almost unique in his treatment of the theme, this time in focusing on the sufferings of poor Catholics under the fines exacted for recusancy:

> Yea, and this law hath been so violently executed, that where poor farmers and husbandmen had but one cow for themselves and many children to live upon, that for their recusancy hath been taken from them. And where both kine and cattle were wanting, they have taken their coverlets, sheets, and blankets from their beds, their victual and poor provision from their houses, not sparing so much as the very glass of their windows when they found nothing else to serve their turns withal. (43)

A reader of the *Supplication* would be able to infer easily enough that its author was a priest. A reader familiar with Southwell's other prose, however, will notice that the claim to specifically priestly authority has gone. When he wrote to his father, he claimed to be "the vicegerent of God" (*Letters,* 19). Now the queen "[supplies] the place and [resembles] the person of almighty God" (*Supplication*, 1), and Southwell speaks to her in the language of equity and justice as the representative of the powerless. The effect is a powerful rebuke to the queen as she is, in the name of the queen she is not. Southwell's voice in the *Supplication* is the source of its authority, and one suspects that only someone who had disciplined himself to accept whatever might be done to him could have written so courageous a book. His interposition of himself between people and Crown at the point where absolute power meets complete powerlessness is a literary prefiguring of the constellation of forces at his execution. The implied shift in his understanding of power, moreover, seems to have been genuine, not merely the consequence of a rhetorical strategy, as his comments on the so-called "bloody question" reveal.

At the heart of the political problem posed by the proclamation, as by all the English anti-Catholic legislation, was the question of Catholic loyalty, ultimately formulated in the notorious "bloody question": "If the Pope do by his Bull or sentence pronounce her Majesty to be deprived, and no lawful Queen, and her subjects to be discharged of their allegiance and obedience unto her; and after, the pope or any other by his appointment and authority, do invade this realm; which part would you take, or which part ought a good subject of England to take?" (Hughes, 3:357–62). This was the "captious question" that people were forced to answer under torture, and to which Southwell gives a plain, though carefully worded reply. We Catholics, he writes, are as ready "to defend your realm, as the Catholic subjects of your majesty's ancestors, or any other prince were, are, or ever shall be . . . we do assure your majesty, that what army soever should come against you, we will rather yield our breasts to be broached by our country swords, than use our swords to th'effusion of our country's blood" (*Supplication,* 35). The second part of that statement could mean that rather than aid an invader, Catholics would choose to be killed as noncombatants by their fellow countrymen. It might also mean that Catholics would rather be killed by their fellow countrymen on suspicion of disloyalty than join an invader. Taken with the first part, however, the whole statement quite definitely says that in Southwell's judgment Catholics would always defend the realm, and that they would rather be massacred than aid an invader. It follows from this position that Southwell accepts completely the authority of the Crown in civil affairs.[18]

R. C. Bald interprets Southwell's answer to the "bloody question" as evidence that when he wrote the *Supplication* he no longer held the intransigent Jesuit view that the Pope was supreme in matters spiritual and temporal, and that Elizabeth was an excommunicated heretic whom it was a Catholic duty to remove. Five years of life as a Catholic in England gave Southwell experience of the English Catholic dilemma: how could one simultaneously be a good Catholic and a good English subject? His answer, Bald believes, implies the development of a national concept of the Catholic Church in England akin to the Gallicanism of the French church (xxi–xxii). Although Bald's view has not met with general approval, it corresponds to contemporary interpretations of the

Supplication. When the quarrel between Jesuits and seculars broke out in England in the later 1590s, Jesuit intransigence on the question of the papal supremacy in England was a subject of disagreement. In 1600, with the connivance of Bishop Bancroft (who was using the quarrel as a means of dividing the English Catholics), the secular party published the *Supplication* secretly under the date 1595 in order to embarrass the Jesuits. Unfortunately, the publication proved even more embarrassing to the government, who suppressed the book and hanged those responsible for distributing it). So it came about, as Bald observes, that what is to a modern reader the "noblest element" in the *Supplication,* Southwell's understanding of the need to reconcile loyalty to church and state, proved an embarrassment to the Jesuits and his former superior, Garnet. That is why the Jesuits tried to suppress the *Supplication,* and why their opponents printed it (xxii).

Southwell's prose reveals a development of spirit, rather than of style, which one can summarize by saying that in the *Supplication,* the claims of love, in this case love of his country and its people, took priority over the homage owed to civil, perhaps even ecclesiastical, power. In its statement of the rights of conscience, of what Southwell calls "soul rights" (28), against the power of the Crown, the *Supplication* can claim a distinguished place in the history of English civil liberties as well as in the history of English prose.

Chapter Four

Southwell's Poetry: *Saint Peter's Complaint*

The Transmission of Southwell's Poems

Unlike his prose, Southwell's poetry cannot be exactly dated. The only exceptions are a pair of poems thought to be about current events: "Decease release" was evidently prompted by the execution of Mary, Queen of Scots, 8 February 1587, and "I die without desert" may be upon the imprisonment of the Earl of Arundel. It is generally assumed that all the poems preserved and published in England were also written in England during his six years of active life there. The Stonyhurst holograph manuscript, however, includes several Latin poems as well as a draft translation into English of stanzas from Tansillo's *Le lagrime di San Pietro;* there is also John Pitts's testimony that Southwell was writing English poetry at the English College. There is no doubt, therefore, that Southwell was already a poet in Rome. It is a virtual certainty that when he landed in England in 1586, he had some English poems with him. Although we do not know exactly when he began writing poetry, we do know when he stopped: after his arrest, 26 June 1592, he had no access to writing materials. During his imprisonment, Henry Garnet was able to transmit a breviary to him; when Garnet recovered it after Southwell's death, he examined it thoroughly for any sign of an inscription, and found only the words "Jesus" and "My God, and my all" scratched with a pin (Janelle, 69).

Wherever and whenever they were written, the poems reach the modern reader through two channels of transmission. In 1595, very soon after Southwell's execution, the publisher John Wolfe issued the first edition of his poems, consisting of *Saint Peter's Complaint* and 12 of the short lyrics. A second edition, which followed immediately, contained another eight lyrics. Later in the same year, another publisher, John Busby, brought out a further collection of 22 short poems under the title *Moeoniae.* The 1602 edition of *Saint Peter's Complaint* included another seven poems. Southwell's name does not appear on these books; *Saint*

Peter's Complaint bears no indication of authorship, and *Moeoniae* has only the initials "R. S." on the title page. Nonetheless, his authorship of the books was an open secret, and the publishers were naturally careful not to attract official attention by printing any obstreperously Catholic poems. From approximately one or two generations after Southwell until modern times, these censored, selective texts were the only generally accessible source of the poetry.

The other channel of transmission is provided by the group of manuscripts already discussed above in connection with *Triumphs over Death.* They represent a vigorous stream of manuscript distribution reaching back into Southwell's own lifetime, and continuing well into the seventeenth century. They all reproduce the same 52 lyrics in substantially the same order. One of them (BL MS Additional 10422) includes a text of *Saint Peter's Complaint,* a second manuscript of which survives in a commonplace book written out by a Catholic copyist called Peter Mowle.[1] None of these manuscripts is holograph, although the best and oldest of them, the Stonyhurst or Waldegrave manuscript, on the evidence of paper and handwriting, could have been copied in the 1590s. As Nancy Pollard Brown suggests, the copyists were Catholics, and the collection of poems may have had almost the status of relics for them (*Poems,* xciii). The manuscripts, however, disappeared from view until the nineteenth century when first Turnbull (1856) used BL MS Additional 10442, and then Grosart (1872) based his edition upon the Waldegrave Manuscript at Stonyhurst, believing that it contained corrections in Southwell's own hand.

The modern rediscovery of the manuscript traditions has naturally tended to project back upon Southwell's own lifetime our perception of two streams of transmission, one authentically Catholic and devotional, the other inauthentically selective, even commercial. What, then, were Southwell's intentions as a poet? What were his readers' expectations? Is the authentic Southwell, as represented by the manuscripts, an almost exclusively didactic and devotional Catholic poet, as his editor, Nancy Pollard Brown, evidently believes? Or did he compose poetry on religious themes for a wider audience, represented by the readership of his printed texts, that was at least as interested in literature as in devotion?

At some point in his ministry (presumably later rather than earlier) Southwell prepared a collection of his short poems to which he prefixed a prose letter, "The author to his loving cousin," and a prefatory poem "To the reader." No copy of this original collection now exists. Southwell also went some way towards preparing *Saint Peter's Complaint* for distribution, and perhaps—like the *Funeral Tears*—for printing; that poem too is prefaced by a poem to the reader. After Southwell's arrest, Brown hypothesizes, an associate compiled a collection of the 52 lyrics, including the prefatory letter and poem, and thus provided a "matrix" that underlies the surviving manuscript collections. Furthermore, she surmises that John Wolfe's first printed edition was based upon (1) a manuscript of *Saint Peter's Complaint* and (2) an incomplete manuscript collection of the lyrics, possibly but not necessarily Southwell's own. In the case of Busby's collection, *Moeoniae,* she believes that the choice of poems "strongly suggests" that he used a copy of the compilation of 52 lyrics (lxxi). On the basis of this reasoning, Brown argues that the publishers selected poems for predominantly literary and commercial reasons from collections put together and preserved, in the first place by the author, for religious and didactic reasons. And she believes very strongly, but on grounds never really made clear, that "Southwell's original gift of poems [to his cousin] did not comprise the group of fifty-two lyrics" (xciii). Thus, in his editor's opinion we find divided interests and intentions at the source of the transmission of Southwell's poetry: on the one hand, commercial publishers and curious buyers; on the other, pious copyists and devotional readers.

In the beginning, the transmission of Southwell's poems was probably a more unified phenomenon than his editor allows. In the first place, although Wolfe seems to have chosen the 12 lyrics in his first edition at random, they are all from the 52-lyric collection. They seem to have been chosen rapidly, but in a way that preserves signs of their original order. The first six are in order except for a reversal of the adjoining pair "Look home" and "Times go by turns" (nos. 43, 44). The next group of three consists of two poems from the 14-poem sequence on Mary and Jesus, plus "A child my choice"; again, they are in order. The last three, from the end of the manuscript, are slightly out of order: "Content and rich" (51), "Loss in delays" (45), and "Love's servile lot" (46). There is no reason not to believe that these poems came from the same collection of 52 that we now have in the manuscripts. The eight lyrics added to the second edition all come from the last part of this collection, and they are in order. It looks very much as though Wolfe, like Busby, used the same collection of lyrics that we have now in the manuscripts, and that it therefore existed well before Wolfe printed his edition. As for the collection itself, the striking thing about it is the constancy with which the copyists preserved the number and the order of the poems. Was it Southwell's own?

Brown advances no clear argument against this possibility, except that the compiler made the mistake of treating "New heaven, new war" as a single poem (xciv). If he did so, however, then he also gave it a mistaken name, since the poem's first four stanzas are quite clearly about the "new heaven," and its second four are about the "new war." If we are to divide the poem, we must also divide the title.[2] A compiler as careful to preserve the order and integrity of his original, as Brown says, will hardly have made so drastic a mistake. Brown is also very skeptical of the authenticity of the translation of Aquinas' Corpus Christi hymn as "An holy hymn." The presence of a bogus item in the collection would rule out the possibility that Southwell compiled it; but Brown's judgment is necessarily a subjective one. There is no evidence against Southwell's authorship.

There is one major manuscript whose contents, postdating Wolfe's edition, definitely represent a unified conception of the poems' transmission. This is a manuscript formerly called the Harmsworth manuscript, now in the Folger Shakespeare Library. It is a hybrid, whose first owner made it by joining a made-up copy of Wolfe's first edition to his own supplementary collection of the lyrics. These, omitting the ones already included in Wolfe's volume, follow exactly the order of the 52-lyric collection, except that the two topical poems, "Decease release" and "I die without desert" are placed at the end. Its compiler added two poems to the sequence on Mary and Jesus, and he added 12 otherwise unknown poems to the end of the collection. The manuscript also includes the Earl of Arundel's "A Fourfold Meditation," correctly attributed to him, as well as 14 poems by Henry Vaux. Evidently, this manuscript's compiler was well supplied with materials emanating from the Vaux and Arundel families whom Southwell knew. Working after the appearance of Wolfe's edition, although he was keen to make his collection complete, with one exception he did not feel bound to respect the order of the manuscript collection. The exception is his correction of Wolfe's displacement of two poems from the sequence of poems on the Virgin and Jesus. Brown dislikes the manuscript because of its compiler's "irresponsibility" (li) in editing his texts, and she is hesitant to accept the additional poems as Southwell's.[3]

The interest of the manuscript's role in the transmission of Southwell's poems is that its compiler made no distinction between print and manuscript; in fact, he went out of his way to make his own additions as much like a printed book as possible. He was obviously a Catholic, but the laborious editorial "irresponsibility" of which Brown disapproves reveals a real, if sometimes less than expert, interest in the wording of the poetry.

Southwell prepared his own texts for dissemination, if not always for actual publication, and his collection of lyrics underlies both the manuscript tradition and the published texts. As the additions to the Harmsworth manuscript prove, Southwell did not include in his collection everything he had written, and the Harmsworth compiler may have been going against Southwell's wishes when he made his additions to the list of poems. When this well-informed and well-supplied Catholic allowed Wolfe's disturbance of the poems' order to stand in his own manuscript, he also registered an implicit disagreement with Brown's opinion that "the fifty-two lyrics have been arranged with sensitive awareness of the place of each in a framework of training in the spiritual life" (xcix). He did not, that is, concede any special devotional or religious authority to the manuscripts' order or contents.

In conclusion, one can suggest, therefore, that although Southwell may have been responsible either for the order of the lyrics in the manuscripts or for the idea that there should be an order, neither his publishers nor the well-equipped, industrious Catholic who made the Harmsworth manuscript thought that there was any intrinsic significance in the order itself, always excepting the sequence on Mary and Jesus. The collection's chief principle of arrangement is grouping by subject matter. The manuscript copyists who preserved the order of the poems so carefully may have done so because they thought it was Southwell's order, not because it was a significant order. There is no evidence that any of these people felt bound to read or use the poems in order, and if we turn to Southwell's own prefatory letter and poems, we shall find nothing there about the order of the poems either. The one suggestion he makes about the reception of his poems is that people might like to sing them. Otherwise, as with *Funeral Tears,* he challenges his contemporaries to write poems about religion and virtue, and leaves no doubt that he will cheerfully enter into competition with them. On balance, modern readers can feel confident that in reading the poems selectively and individually rather than as parts of a didactic or devotional scheme, they are following the lead of the first publishers, the Harmsworth compiler, and, probably, Robert Southwell himself. To judge from the construction of *Saint Peter's Complaint,* Southwell is more likely to have arranged a collection of short poems spatially, allotting a central place to a poem or group of poems, rather than attempting to place them all in a linear and didactic scheme.

Southwell's Style

When C. S. Lewis attempted to place Southwell historically, he concluded that Southwell "modestly but firmly refused to take any notice, as a poet, of the period in which he was living" (544). Louis Martz explains Southwell's stylistic eccentricity by pointing out that when he and Garnet landed in England in 1586, *Tottell's Miscellany* had yet to go through two more editions (1587, 1589), and Watson's *Hekatompathia or Passionate Century of Love* had just appeared (1582), as had the *Handful of Pleasant Delights* (1584). *The Paradise of Dainty Devices* (1576) was the most popular anthology at the time, going into six editions between 1576 and 1590. In Martz's view, this kind of verse provided the basis of Southwell's poetry, except that he brought back with him from Rome the reforming preoccupations of the Counter-Reformation, set out in his prefaces and prefatory poems. As a Jesuit, he also brought the art of meditation with him, and his only English precursor seems to be another Jesuit, Donne's uncle, Jasper Heywood, in two poems added to the 1585 edition of *The Paradise of Dainty Devices:* "The complaint of a sorrowful soul," and "Alluding his state to the prodigal child."[4]

What Lewis called the "Tottelian," or "drab," style dominates many of Southwell's lyrics, especially the gnomic and moralizing poems, such as "Times go by turns," "Loss in delays," and "Life's death love's life," and it can appear in almost any poem at any moment. His best poems, stanzas, and lines, however, are not in this style at all, although it is easier to recognize the characteristically Southwellian style than to describe it in the abstract:

> Ah life, sweet drop, drowned in a sea of showers,
> A flying good, posting to doubtful end
> (*Saint Peter's Complaint,* ll. 85–86)

> Behold the father, is his daughter's son:
> The bird that built the nest, is hatched therein.
> ("The Nativity of Christ," ll. 1–2)

> Thy ghostly beauty offered force to God,
> It chained him in the links of tender love.
> ("At home in heaven," ll. 7–8)

Each of these three pairs of lines is dominated by a strong metaphor, and two of them are apostrophic, a figure that often imparts a numinous quality to a statement, drawing attention to its mystery and power. The lines are also full of activity; the most important meaning is in the verbal forms, "drowned," "posting," "built," "is hatched," "offered," and "chained." The language is a plain, economical English in natural word order. To quote A. C. Partridge, "The purity of Southwell's un-Latinized English is due to the condensation of his sentences and the simplicity of his rhythms, dominated by syllables containing liquid consonants. The language is so clear and precise that it seldom needs glossing."[5] The resulting style gives Southwell more in common with Donne and his seventeenth-century successors in both verse and prose than with his sixteenth-century contemporaries. Like the metaphysical style, Southwell's conveys the sound and energy of the speaking voice. The verse can be declamatory, even dramatic; at moments one is not too far from the great pulpits of the age, even from the stage of the Globe theater.

Such a style engages the reader in mental dialogue with the poem. Joseph D. Scallon, in one of the most interesting and important monographs on Southwell, relates the dramatic quality of his poetry to the aesthetics of the Counter-Reformation:

> As the Counter Reform began to take hold, the self-contained perfection to be found in the works of the masters of the High Renaissance was replaced by the deliberately elongated and distorted compositions of Mannerist and Baroque artists who force the viewer to look for the truth behind the picture and form a judgement on it. The new styles draw the viewer into the scene depicted and demand that he share the emotions of the original situation. This shift in the relationship between artifact and audience from passive admiration of classic perfection to active participation in the emotion of the event, which Baroque and Mannerist artists sought to evoke, must have seemed to the early Jesuits a providential development. Here was a working out in art of an important aspect of Ignatian ascetical practice, the so-called composition of place.[6]

As Scallon goes on to suggest, therefore, within the Church the liturgical and architectural consequence of the aesthetic change was the building of well-lit churches without choir screens, in which the high altar, magnificently treated in imagery and architectural detail, is the focal point. Such churches are designed to engage the congregation's imagination and intellect in the unfolding action of the mass as the central act of worship. In Southwell's literary art, the central artistic means he uses to engage his reader is the metaphorical conceit that, however grotesque or surprising, he nearly always deploys in a context of lucid English syntax and vocabulary, as in, "A sea will scantly rinse my ordured soul"

(*Saint Peter's Complaint,* l.77). Placed against his Roman and Counter-Reformation background, and read selectively, Southwell's poetry was as innovative in Elizabethan England as his prose, and it is misleading to stress too much his Tottelian or "drab" poetic ancestry.

One of Southwell's earliest biographers, Diego de Yepez, said that while Southwell was at the English College, he "applied himself with much diligence to the study of his native tongue, which he had already nearly forgotten, because he left England very young" (Janelle, 32). Several modern commentators adduce Yepez's words to provide a history of the first stages of Southwell's writing, and also to explain the idiosyncrasies of his style, especially its marked difference from contemporary English work.[7] It is true that all daily conversation at the English College, as in the universities of Oxford and Cambridge, was in Latin, equally true that at some periods of his education Southwell would have heard little if any English at all. Since there are stories of English dons who lost facility in writing and speaking English after years of university life,[8] it seems on the face of it possible that Southwell might have had some difficulty with English. Yet he was never long out of touch with intensely patriotic young Englishmen like himself, or, therefore, with his language. The students at the English College were in constant touch with political and cultural developments in England. Although most of Southwell's writing in his Roman years was either Latin or Italian, he probably never stopped writing English entirely, and when he began writing seriously in English at the English College, his choice of models probably had no connection with his facility, but rather with his religious and cultural allegiances.

Spenser's *Shepherd's Calendar* was published in 1579, seven years before Southwell went to England, and the only signs in Southwell's poetry of the English Renaissance style associated with Spenser and Sidney and the poets of Southwell's own generation who followed them are signs of rejection such as the well-known lines from the poem prefacing *Saint Peter's Complaint:*

> Christ's thorn is sharp, no head his garland wears:
> Still finest wits are stilling Venus' rose. (ll. 15–16)

The new Renaissance English style was too closely associated with either a Protestant or a paganizing humanism for a recusant writer to adopt it, especially a Jesuit poet. Fascinating evidence of this probability is to be found in a curious poem by Anthony Copley, *A Fig for Fortune,* published in 1596, and dedicated to the Catholic nobleman, Anthony Browne, Viscount Montague.

Copley was Southwell's cousin on his mother's side. He entered the English College at Rome in October 1584 and received minor orders from the bishop of St. Asaph; but life at the college proved uncongenial to him, and he left in 1586, "because he did not wish to remain."[9] A letter from Southwell to Agazzari of December 1986, written in the aftermath of the Babington Plot arrests, reports that Anthony's mother and brother were imprisoned, and transmits a message to him from his mother begging him to stay in Rome (Pollen 1908, 318). He was something of a scapegrace, though Southwell seems to have been very fond of him. Devlin reports that at the college he caused a stir by appearing in the pulpit to preach with a rose between his teeth (257). Back home in England he was one of the people Southwell visited, as Topcliffe reports in the letter he wrote to the queen describing his plans to torture Southwell: "Young Anthony Copley the most desperate youth that liveth and some others be most familiar with Southwell. Copley did shoot at a gentleman the last summer, and killed an ox with a musket, and in Horsham church threw his dagger at the parish clerk and stuck it in a seat in the church. There liveth not the like in England for sudden attempts."[10] After Robert's death Copley associated himself with the secular party in the appellant controversy, and became embroiled in the Bye and Main plots.

Copley's little allegory of about 2,000 lines in six-line stanzas seems to be a response to the first book of *The Faerie Queene,* and it is undoubtedly autobiographical.[11] Its hero is an unhappy subject of the realm of Elizium and its queen, Eliza. First, the spirit of Cato tempts him to suicide; then Revenge (a Machiavellian who believes in "policy") encourages him to be revenged on his enemies. With daylight, his allegorical horse called Melancholy faints under him, and he mounts another, called Good Desire, which brings him to Mount Sion. There he meets the hermit Catechrysius, who converts and catechizes him and brings him to the temple, where the porter, forbidden to admit Elizians, admits him to the service as a catechumen (sig. I4v).

While this service is taking place, Doblessa and her forces attack: "She had no altar nor no sacrament / No ceremony, nor oblation, / Her school was cavil, and truthless babblement" (sig. K3v). "The high Sacrificator" confirms the hero, and weeps for joy "that an *Elizian* / Would come to be of his Metropolitan," while Catechrysius prays "O that Eliza were / A Sionite to see this gear" (sig. K4v). While the war with Doblessa is going on, some Sionites devote themselves to worship and devotion, and some to scholarship. But there are others:

> And of such brave adventurous Sionites
> As *Doblessa* could by hook or crook intrap
> They died the death, and suffered all the spites
> That rage and rascal wit could jointly rap,
> Subject they were to dreadful persecution
> By public edict, and false brethrens' treason. (sig. L2v)

Some of Doblessa's people, thinking they have won the war, spread false news; others, seeing the true issue of events, join the Sionites against whom, it has been prophesied, the gates of hell will not prevail (sig. L4). When the fighting is over, a virgin appears in the sky, attended by the court of heaven. This, of course, is Mary as queen of heaven: "She was the genium of high Hierusalem" (sig. M1v). The hero at first thinks she is Eliza, but Catechrysius sets him straight about this, upon which, with his lap full of roses, he finds himself back home in Elizium.

Sion is the Catholic Church, Elizium and Eliza are England and its queen, and Doblessa, Copley's answer to Spenser's Duessa, is Protestantism in all its iconoclastic fury. The "brave adventurous Sionites" are the missionary priests. The poem is a fascinating account of the state of mind of a young Catholic in Elizabeth's England, showing how he rejects various fashionable alternatives to the faith—melancholy, epicureanism, and Machiavellianism. Copley also tries, however clumsily, to distinguish between the felicity of England and the crown as a good to which temporal loyalty and affection are due, and the happiness of life within the Church, to which a different loyalty is owed.

It is significant that a poem that is an explicit counterstatement to the first book of *The Faerie Queene*, showing that life is not at all the same for a young Catholic as it is for a young Protestant, is written in a style completely unlike Spenser's. Like Southwell's, Copley's style is based on Tottel and *The Mirror for Magistrates,* although his diction can be eccentrically Latinate, with words like "pectoral" for "breast" (sig. B1), and "my upper albitude" (sig. B1v) for "my upper half clothed in white," and it can have a kind of colloquial force from time to time: "Fie on those loutish grouthead Jobbernowles / That slander Nature with their Modicums" (sig. B3). However clumsy the result of this curious stylistic mixture, Copley intended to separate himself from his contemporaries, and to modify in his own way the earlier styles he inherited; one concludes that the

Recusants' refusals evidently covered literature as well as churchgoing. Copley, of course, was a very minor, even amateur poet. In Southwell's case, his public challenges to contemporaries to change their literary ways encompassed both style and subject matter. That being so, Southwell was really challenging the whole literary culture of the period.

> Profane conceits and feigning fits I fly,
> Such lawless stuff doth lawless speeches fit:
> With *David* verse to virtue I apply,
> Whose measure best with measured words doth sit:
> It is the sweetest note that man can sing,
> When grace in virtue's key tunes nature's string.
> ("To the Reader," ll. 13–18, *Poems,* 2)

Read as a stylistic manifesto, that stanza calls for an elevated but plain and natural poetic style which, by implication, is quite different from the available styles of the age.

Saint Peter's Complaint

Southwell's only long poem, *Saint Peter's Complaint,* a monologue in which St. Peter expresses his remorse for betraying Christ, raises all these questions of transmission, intention, and style. The poem survives in two manuscripts, one in the British Library (Additional Manuscript 10422), the other at Oscott College (Peter Mowle's commonplace book), and in the series of editions inaugurated by John Wolfe in 1595. Since both the manuscripts and the first edition make the mistake of moving 16 stanzas (ll. 235–330) to a place later in the poem (*Poems,* lv), they must be related through a common source containing the mistake that was different from Southwell's own holograph manuscript. As the prefatory poem, "The Author to the Reader," indicates, Southwell prepared this poem for publication, and the relationship of the printed and manuscript witnesses to the text suggests that there were several manuscripts in circulation before the first edition appeared. Indeed, the poem's circulation may have begun well before Southwell's arrest. If it did so, then according to Brown (xc–xci), the text was still not in its final form, but needed further revision. In any case, the channels of transmission in print and manuscript have a common source, and as the prefatory poem states very clearly, Southwell addressed his poem to a readership of fellow writers, and not primarily to a solely Catholic or devotional readership:

> License my single pen to seek a fere,
> You heavenly sparks of wit, shew native light:
> Cloud not with misty loves your orient clear,
> Sweet flights you shoot; learn once to level right.
> Favor my wish, well wishing works no ill:
> I move the suit, the grant rests in your will.
> ("The Author to the Reader," ll. 19–24)

Like *Mary Magdalen's Funeral Tears, Saint Peter's Complaint* was meant to be a challenge to other writers to reform literary taste.

Southwell's interest in the subject of St. Peter, and the beginnings of his poem, are traceable to his time at the English College. There are actually four compositions by Southwell called "Saint Peter's Complaint," all interrelated. First, there is the long poem itself. Then there is a poem with the same title in the manuscript collection of lyric poems, consisting of 12 stanzas from the long poem, evidently representing an earlier state of the text. There is yet another poem with the title, in four-line stanzas, found among the additional poems in the Harmsworth manuscript; this seems to be an even earlier version. Finally, the Stonyhurst holograph manuscript contains four pages of a rough draft of a poem called "Peeter Playnt" (or "Peter Plaint"), and this version seems to be the earliest of all.

Herbert Thurston was the first scholar to identify the source of all these poems as Luigi Tansillo's *Le lagrime di San Pietro,* a popular Italian poem of the period. He thought Southwell only knew a brief early draft of the *lagrime* (tears), and that it merely gave him a general idea for his own work.[12] Mario Praz, however, was able to show that the draft called "Peter Plaint" was "a crude attempt . . . rather than a serious one" at actually translating some stanzas from the fragmentary first version of Tansillo's poem, first published in 1560. Even more interesting, however, was Praz's discovery that there were also close parallels between the fragmentary version of Tansillo and the 12-stanza version of *Saint Peter's Complaint.*[13] (Praz did not know of the existence of the Harmsworth version.) Praz's findings showed that Southwell began the *Complaint* in Italy, and that he might even have brought quite a large part of the poem with him to England already written. Devlin sums up the probabilities: "He had begun work on the Italian original as early as 1584, and he kept on refurbishing it at intervals" (258). The poem and its theme must have been a continual preoccupation for him, even though he began it at the same time as *Mary Magdalen's Funeral Tears* and with the same motivation.

Tansillo's poem, written to make amends for the author's own licentious life and writing, originated the Counter Reformation literature of tears and repentance. The *lagrime* began to circulate in manuscript in 1559; this version, printed in 1560, consisted of only 42 *ottava rima* stanzas, which continued to circulate in print and manuscript until 1585. In that year an enormously extended version of the poem appeared. Southwell seems only to have known the short version. Moreover, in following Tansillo, he used only the lyrical, soliloquizing portions of the poem, and his own poem is entirely lyrical. His motive in taking up the theme of Peter's guilt and repentance, writes Devlin, "was frankly an apostolic one: to attract imaginative souls to repentance and the life of the spirit" (259). Brown has developed this point in some detail, arguing that the poem's structure represents Tridentine teaching on the sacrament of penance, a contested subject between Protestants and Catholics: "Southwell compresses time and place into the indistinguishable present[14] immediately following the betrayal, and the words are those of Peter, as if he were in the presence of a priest at the tribunal of penance; in this imaginative development all those elements contained within the sacrament of the church are set out in order: contrition, confession, the desire to make satisfaction, and the reception of absolution."[15] The first part of the poem shows Peter's remorse, the essential first stage to an act of penance, and Brown suggests that the line "Baptize thy spotted soul in weeping dew" (l. 18) is a specific reference to the sacrament of penance, defined at the Council of Trent as "a laborious kind of baptism" (Brown 1966, 6). Southwell's construction of the stages of Peter's suffering as he works his way towards contrition, Brown believes, is actually based on the second exercise of the first week of the Ignatian *Spiritual Exercises,* a formal meditation on "our sins." She concludes that "the structure of the sacrament of penance gives the poem a unity of form and a profound meaning" (11).

Lest this all sound too cut-and-dried, it should be added that Brown also points out that Peter has to seek reconciliation without a priest, since at the time of his mourning, "the way of reconciliation offered by Christ had not yet been opened to the sinner." For Peter, then, "the way to a truly contrite heart is a tortuous and solitary way of self-examination, stormed by emotional crises which at times threaten to hurl him into despair." Consequently, the poem can be read as a private, inward rite of reconciliation for an alienated soul deprived of the ministrations of a priest. By this reading, Peter, interpreted analogically, would stand not only for the isolated Catholic without access to the sacraments, but more specifically for the Catholic apostate, of whom there were many in Elizabethan England.[16] And of course, the temptation to join Peter in betraying Christ must have been continually present to Southwell's own imagination; who could tell what might happen in the aftermath of capture and torture? In suggesting that the poem owed its popularity to its doctrinal purpose, though, Brown does not allow for the more interesting possibility that Southwell's personal engagement in the theme gave his treatment of it an intensity that no versified doctrine could have. In fact, like other didactic and utilitarian readings of Southwell, Brown's rather formulaic account of the poem hardly mentions its aesthetic and affective power. Yet as Devlin notes, "The long section on the Sacred Eyes of our Redeemer, in which [Southwell] plays over theological depths with a sensuous ardour that cedes nothing to Crashaw" was a "quarry for poets of his own and succeeding generations as late as Andrew Marvell" (259). Given the power and subtlety of Southwell's penetration of Peter's psychology, many of his non-Catholic contemporaries might have found in reading the *Complaint* an aesthetic substitute for churchly ministrations. If that were so, then this Jesuit poem would have appealed strongly to a wide range of readers quite independently of any doctrinal position it implied.

In any case, the forms of a meditation, of a sacrament, and of a poem are very different things, as are the purposes to which they are directed. The *Complaint* has its own form, which is surprisingly similar to the form of its much longer prose companion, *Mary Magdalen's Funeral Tears.* Work on both began with translation from a source, soon abandoned as Southwell turned to his own version of the theme, which in both cases is provided by a study of a mind in the grip of powerful emotion. He arranges the material on a narrative framework, but the narrative element is reduced to a minimum, in the *Funeral Tears* to the gospel narrative itself, and in the *Complaint* to extremely brief paraphrases of the synoptic gospels' narrative of Peter's betrayal, appearing for the most part as Peter remembers the events, not in the order of their original happening. At line 103, for instance, Peter remembers the sin itself: "I worse than both, for nought denied him thrice"; and a few stanzas later, at line 125, he recalls how, as the gospel narrative puts it, he "began to curse and to swear that he knew not the man" (Matthew 26.74): "My oaths, were stones: my cruel tongue the sling: / My God, the mark: at which my spight did fling." The maidservant whose question caused his first denial does not appear until line 150: "A puff of woman's breath bred all my fear." The sum total of such narrative lines would hardly make up six whole stanzas. The result, as Helen White writes, "is . . . a dramatic thing, a penetration by the poet into the consciousness of another being."[17] Southwell seems to have assumed that his readers would know the story, as they would know Peter's later history, and that they would therefore easily perceive that the story was the organizing basis of the poem. It should be added, too, that as Brian Oxley has suggested, a reader should perhaps have in mind the narrative of Christ's death and passion as well (Oxley, 337).

Since the narrative element follows an order of memory and association, however, instead of chronology, it does not by itself give the poem a readily grasped formal shape. Southwell provides this by a clear spatial arrangement of his poem's parts. There are 132 stanzas, a number probably chosen because it is a multiple of 11 and 12. In numerological lore it was very well-known that 11 was the number of sin, being deficient by one of the number of grace and salvation, 12.[18] The poem is divided exactly into two parts by the 20-stanza apostrophe to the eyes of Christ, occupying stanzas 56–75, which thus becomes the poem's center. Whether a reader actually knows the numbers or not, it is impossible to read the poem without experiencing the centricity of Christ in its construction; similarly, it is impossible not to see that in general Peter's temptation, sin, and remorse occupy the poem's first half, his sorrowful contrition the second half. Of course, the poem's fundamental units are the six-line stanzas, in Southwell's hands an epigrammatic form of which he became an accomplished master. Southwell arranges his stanzas in groups of different sizes, from the single-stanza address to John and James (ll. 601–6) to the 20-stanza group devoted to the eyes of Christ. The stanzas are not linked by an argument, but by the common theme of remorse and the fact that Peter's mind is thinking them. Movement from one group to another can be quite arbitrary, as when Peter switches from a comparison of himself to Absolom (sts. 91–92, ll. 541–52) to a three-stanza address to the Holy Innocents (ll. 553–70). Peter's own explanation of the form of his monologue is that "Sad subject of my sin hath stored my mind / With everlasting matter of complaint," and his poem, he says, is an "endless alphabet" of lamentation (ll. 37–39). Reading it, therefore, is more like listening to variations on a bass or ground, that favorite Elizabethan instrumental form, than like following a process or a narrative, even though a basis of narrative may be implied. In fact, the lack of a linear scheme of progression in the poem suggests that each of the stanza groups, with the exception of the central one on the eyes of Christ, could be regarded as a "tear" in the flood of lamentation. In its form, the *Complaint* has more in common with Crashaw's "The Weeper" than with a contemporary complaint such as Daniel's *Rosamond.*

Thus, just as readers of the *Funeral Tears* would have found an extremely original work, both in style and content, erected upon a familiar base, so with the *Complaint:* readers accustomed to *The Mirror for Magistrates* and the poems in Tottel's *Songs and Sonnets* would find a familiar genre and style turned into something entirely new to them.

The newness did not come to Southwell all at once. The 12 stanzas of the version in the lyric collection occur, with one exception, among the first 29 stanzas of the long version, and they are noticeably lacking in the concentration and energy of its best passages. In incorporating them into the long text, Southwell performed some revisions. Although he could not entirely transform the flat, expository rhetoric of his early stanzas into the drama of the later ones, he could certainly improve it. One such revised stanza is number 17, lines 97–102. First, the original:

> Was life so dear and Christ become so base,
> I of so great, God of so small account:
> That Peter needs must follow Judas' race,
> And all the Jews in cruelty surmount?
> Yet Judas deemed thirty pence his price:
> I, worse than he, for nought denied him thrice.

In that version, the very organization of the stanza is inert. The antitheses of the first two lines are clumsy. "Judas' race" is a vague expression, "the Jews in cruelty" is a crude stereotype, and the concluding couplet seems unprepared for. Now the revision:

> And could I rate so high a life so base?
> Did fear with love cast so uneven[19] accompt,
> That for this goal I should run Judas' race,
> And Caiphas' rage in cruelty surmount?
> Yet they esteemed thirty pence his price:
> I, worse than both, for nought denied him thrice.

The final couplet is now prepared for by the monetary metaphor of the first two lines; the addition of Caiphas makes "both" precise and logical, and "goal" and "run" develop the metaphor of "race."

Such revision is evidence of greatly increased technical mastery of the form itself, a necessary basis for confidence and freedom in expression.

Although the *Complaint* is an uneven work, this may not be because it was never finally revised, as its editor believes, but because the groups of stanzas from which it is constructed were accumulated over time. At its best it is a poem of great power and subtlety, a complex study of a mind anatomizing a sin and its consequences. Southwell's Jesuit training will have taught him to observe psychological processes closely and accurately. The poetic technique he invented to express them in English, in all their range of variation and subtlety, on the other hand, was original.

The narrative basis of the poem is a combination of the accounts of Peter's betrayal given in Matthew 26.69–75, and Luke 22.54–62. Matthew omits Jesus' looking at Peter, and Luke omits Peter's cursing and swearing. Here is Luke's version:

> 54 And apprehending him, they led him to the high priest's house. But Peter followed afar off.
> 55 And when they had kindled a fire in the midst of the hall, and were sitting about it, Peter was in the midst of them.
> 56 Whom when a certain servant maid had seen sitting at the light, and had earnestly beheld him, she said: This man also was with him.
> 57 But he denied him, saying: Woman, I know him not.
> 58 And after a little while, another seeing him, said: Thou also art one of them. But Peter said: O man, I am not.
> 59 And after the space, as it were of one hour, another certain man affirmed, saying: Of a truth, this man was also with him; for he is also a Galilean.
> 60 And Peter said: Man, I know not what thou sayest. And immediately, as he was yet speaking, the cock crew.
> 61 And the Lord turning looked on Peter. And Peter remembered the word of the Lord, as he had said: Before the cock crow, thou shalt deny me thrice.
> 62 And Peter going out, wept bitterly.

For Southwell the fact at the heart of this narrative is that for no acceptable reason at all Peter has betrayed the person he loves most. His sin is a brief act of violence committed in the name of "life" against the one person who stands for an absolute of beauty and virtue in his world, who is everything he believes in, and as such is a part of himself. In a real way, consequently, the *Complaint* is a poem about defeated or betrayed love. "*Christ,* as my God," says Peter, "was templed in my thought" (l. 631).

Out of fear he has knowingly violated that sacred image: "Base fear out of my heart his love unshrined" (l. 195). He acts, too, to preserve a "life" he knows is illusory compared to the good he must lose, an idea expressed through images of a little time gained in exchange for much time lost:

> Ah life, sweet drop, drowned in a sea of sours,
> A flying good, posting to doubtful end:
> Still loosing months and years to gain new hours. (ll. 85–87)

The moment of sin itself is hardly felt as such at all; in the act a kind of death obscures the faculties. The sin committed, however, the sinner awakes to pain, a sense of loss, and a profound, metaphysical wound:

> Shot, without noise: wound without present smart:
> First, seeming light, proving in fine a load,
> Entering with ease, not easily won to part. (ll. 649–51)

The consequences of a sin of this kind upon the sinner are at least threefold. First, there is the desecration of something very highly valued that is part of the self; Peter has "unshrined" Christ from his heart (195). Second, the sinner has desecrated his own soul, which is the temple of the beloved: Peter's soul is now so badly "spotted" (18) that "A sea will scantly rince my ordured soul" (44). Third, the act which seems so brief and so local extends itself through time and space to grow to something of cosmic significance. When Christ looks on Peter after the betrayal, his eyes are whole worlds of paradisal joy from which Peter is now exiled:

> O sacred eyes, the springs of living light,
> The earthly heavens, where Angels joy to dwell:
> How could you deign to view my deathful plight,
> Or let your heavenly beams look on my hell? (ll. 331–34)

As Christ is the center and sum of Peter's life ("I lost all that I had, and had the most" [l. 505]), so the 20-stanza apostrophe to the eyes of Christ is at the numerical center of the poem, and the eyes themselves are the center and sum of the world. As Brian Oxley, who has also noticed the centric construction of the poem, points out, Peter's world is not only centered upon Christ as the microcosmic sum of all beauty and all value, but equally upon love as the redeeming, centering principle of life (Oxley, 339):

O gracious spheres, where love the Center is,
A native place for our self-loaden souls:
The compass, love, a cope that none can miss:
The motion, love that round about us rolls.
O spheres of love, whose Center, cope, and motion,
Is love of us, love that invites devotion.

O little worlds, the sums of all the best,
Where glory, heaven, God, sun: all virtues, stars:
Where fire, a love that next to heaven doth rest,
Air, light of life, that no distemper mars:
The water, grace, whose seas, whose springs, whose showers,
Clothe nature's earth, with everlasting flowers. (ll. 403–14)

Peter's sin has driven him from this centered cosmos of coherence and love to become an exiled wanderer in psychic space: "I outcast from these worlds exiled roam" (l. 421). Worst of all, he has become hell to himself: "The sugared poison now hath wrought so well: / That thou hast made me to my self a hell" (ll. 671–72). Peter thus becomes the thing he has done as well as the place of his doing it. (He also calls the firelit hall in the high priest's house "this earthly hell" [l. 229].)

A sympathetic reader will soon notice that one consequence of Southwell's treatment of his subject is that there develops from the conceited style itself a continual, reciprocal movement from the concrete to the metaphorical, with the result that the conceits are not merely an element in a decorative rhetoric: they are a faithful translation into symbolic images of the moral reality being represented. For instance, when Peter says, "A sea will scantly rinse my ordured soul" (l. 44), he is thinking of someone trying to wash badly soiled linen, and that homely action is charged with moral significance for him; yet when he goes on to say, three lines later, "These stains are deep: few drops, take out no such," we hardly conceive of the stains as concrete at all because the concept "stain" has become moral rather than physical. A variant form of the image appears later in the poem:

O Bethlehem cisterns, David's most desire,
From which my sins like fierce Philistines keep,
To fetch your drops what champion should I hire,
That I therein my withered heart may steep. (ll. 427–30)

The first three lines have a literary source in patristic allegorizing of a passage in the Old Testament, 2 Kings 23.15–16. King David longs for "a drink of the water out of the cistern, that is in Bethlehem, by the gate," whereupon "three valiant men broke through the camp of the Philistines, and drew water out of the cistern of Bethlehem." The Bethlehem water was interpreted as a figure or type of Christ. Perhaps, had Southwell fully developed this allegory, the three valiant champions who rout the Philistines, or sins, that prevent Peter from drinking Bethlehem's living waters would be his three faculties of memory, understanding, and will. The fourth line of the passage, however, brings into the learned, entirely literary biblical allegory an image based upon the very homely activity of soaking dried meat in water. The sudden change in the mode of the imagery is surprising, and the homely image itself can seem grotesque in the context, but like the soiled linen of line 44, its violence is proportionate to the speaker's mental distress. The violence of images such as these arises from their incongruity in the context, causing a sharp tension in the reader's mind between the literal and the metaphorical meanings. A musical equivalent would be a completely unprepared change of key. In fact, Southwell's effect is similar to that caused by a parallel phenomenon very common in Elizabethan modal polyphony, the "false relation," which occurs when two vocal or instrumental lines meet in a minor second. The unprepared listener who hears the sharp discord is repelled; the listener who hears the harmonic logic in the converging lines of polyphony is moved in a way for which we have no effective terminology. A similar effect in the poetry of the Spanish Golden Age, I am told, is called *el desgarrón afectivo,* the "affective rift," or "rending."

Southwell treats his conceits as a musician handled his "points" or melodic motifs and phrases. Throughout this long poem, conceits recur, varied in themselves and in relationship to their context, so that the recurrence and patterning of conceits is an important structural principle. Southwell's most important motif is water—seas, rivers, springs, fountains, pools, cisterns, rain, dew, tears, perspiration—which he treats as a symbol of the active principle of remorse and repentance, a means of cleansing, dissolving, softening, and renewing. Water's natural opposites are fire, stone, and its own stony form, ice. So the poem begins, "Launch forth my Soul into a main of tears," and as the monologue proceeds, the conceits provide the theater of action in the reader's mind. The nocturnal setting of Peter's betrayal, with the cold night and the warm, tempting fire, reflects the nature of the sin as much as it sets the scene for it. In Peter's mind the setting is an emblem for hell where, paradoxically, his conscience and will are frozen in the firelight:

> Sharp was the weather in that stormy place,
> Best suiting hearts benumbed with hellish frost,
> Whose crusted malice could admit no grace,
> Where coals were kindled to the warmer's cost.
> Where fear, my thoughts candied with icey cold:
> Heat, did my tongue to perjuries unfold.[20]
>
> O hateful fire (ah that I ever saw it)
> Too hard my heart was frozen for thy force,
> Far hotter flames it did require to thaw it,
> Thy hell resembling heat did freeze it worse.
> O that I rather had congealed to ice,
> Than bought thy warmth at such a damning price. (ll. 247–58)

This is the place, the condition, on which the poem's absolving waters will work, and the betrayal scene has its counterpart in the poem's formal design with the invocation of tears, beginning at stanza 78: "Come sorrowing tears, the offspring of my grief" (463).

St. Peter and Lucrece

In *Saint Peter's Complaint,* Southwell will often remind one of later poets. He anticipates Donne's capacity for close argument in strong, plain English, as in a passage on the eyes of Christ as microcosms of the created world:

> What mixtures these sweet elements do yield,
> Let happy worldlings of those worlds expound,
> But simples are by compounds far excelled,
> Both suit a place, where all best things abound. (ll. 415–18)

His deployment of powerfully (and for some tastes excessively) affective imagery looks forward to Crashaw, as in parts of the apostrophe to Christ's eyes ("O turtle twins all bath'd in virgin's milk" [433]), or in a stanza on the Holy Innocents:

> Sweet roses mixed with Lillies strowed your hearse,
> Death virgin white in martyrs' red did steep:
> Your downy heads both pearls and rubies crowned . . . (ll. 561–63)

Among poems influenced by the *Complaint,* Devlin names Shakespeare's *Rape of Lucrece,* basing his opinion on a number of parallel passages and concluding that "the real debt of Shakespeare . . . would seem to be an inspiration rather than a set of conceits" (272). In particular, he sees an allegorical tendency in *Lucrece:* "The rape becomes an allegory of the violation of a soul by sin" (269); and in working out this reading, he anticipates those Shakespeare scholars who have commented upon what he calls "a rape within a rape" (272). Devlin's case is impressive, although it was weakened for some original readers because he combined it with an argument for a personal acquaintance between Southwell and Shakespeare that the evidence, interesting though it is, will not support.[21]

The list of possible parallels between the two poems is considerably longer than Devlin's few citations suggest, and since *Lucrece* is dated 1593–94, and Southwell did no more writing after June 1592, the influence can only have traveled in one direction.[22] As Devlin says, the poems have in common "any number of similar antitheses and apostrophes" (270), and they share a common storehouse of similes. Shakespeare and Southwell both include a dying swan: "Like solest swan that swims in silent deep, / And never sings but obsequies of death" (*Complaint,* ll. 451–52); "And now this pale swan in her watery nest, / Begins the sad dirge of her certain ending" (*Lucrece,* ll. 1611–12). There is a significant cedar in both poems: "Our cedar now is shrunk into a shrub" (*Complaint,* l. 618); "The cedar stoops not to the base shrub's foot" (*Lucrece,* l. 664). And the paradox of the silent speaker appears in both poems: "Dumb orator that woos with silent deeds" (*Complaint,* l. 236); "Beauty itself doth of itself persuade / The eyes of men without an orator" (*Lucrece,* ll. 29–30).[23] Parallels of this kind are insufficient to prove dependence; they only prove that there was a common poetic currency in circulation at the time.

The more interesting parallels are those that reveal a shared theme and approach. Both poems anatomize a sin committed against someone who stands for absolute beauty and goodness in the sinner's mind. As Christ is "templed" in Peter's thought, so the narrator of *Lucrece* tells us that "within his [Tarquin's] thought her heavenly image sits" (l. 288). Moreover, as Devlin very acutely noticed, the image of the soul as a consecrated virgin inhabiting the temple of the body is an important one in Southwell's poetry (272), so that sin can desecrate both virgin and temple. Peter has "unshrined" (l. 195) the love of Christ from his heart, and brought "his temple to ruin" (l. 633). Similarly Tarquin, raping Lucrece, has desecrated his own soul and sacked her temple: "His soul's fair temple is defaced" (l. 719). For Lucrece too, the rape is a desecration of the soul's temple: "Her house is sack'd, her quiet interrupted, / Her mansion batter'd by the enemy" (ll. 1170–71). As Peter's sin exiles him from the living world of love and joy to wander in the hell of his own being, so Tarquin, "a captive victor that hath lost in gain," knowing that he has destroyed his own soul, carries away from his crime "the wound that nothing healeth, / The scar that will despite of cure remain" (ll. 730–32). Both sinners know, too, that the kind of life they are choosing when they sin is a delusion. "Ah life," says Peter, "sweet drop, drowned in a sea of sours, / A flying good, posting to doubtful end . . . / A flower, a play, a blast, a shade, a dream, / A living death, a never turning stream" (ll. 85–86, ll. 95–96). And Tarquin: "What win I if I gain the thing I seek? / A dream, a breath, a froth of fleeting joy?" (ll. 211–12). At the moral heart of both characters' experience, too, is the revelation of their sin in its true appearance:

> Bewitching evil, that hides death in deceits,
> Still borrowing lying shapes to mask thy face,
> Now I know the deciphering of thy sleights,
> A cunning dearly bought with loss of grace. (*Complaint,* ll. 667–70)

> O deeper sin than bottomless conceit
> Can comprehend in still imagination!
> Drunken desire must vomit his receipt
> Ere he can see his own abomination. (*Lucrece,* ll. 701–4)

The last we hear of Tarquin, as he steals out of the poem into the dark night, is that he is a penitent, "a heavy convertite" (l. 743).

Devlin wishes us to believe that in writing *Lucrece,* Shakespeare was responding to Southwell's call for a more serious, moral poetry. The most specific textual parallel between Shakespeare and Southwell, while it may tend to support Devlin's view, undoubtedly suggests that Shakespeare took a strong writerly and literary interest in Southwell's work. The parallel involves the rather unusual use of "spotted" in a moral and religious sense. It occurs twice in the *Complaint:* "spotted soul" (l. 18) and "spotted fame" (l. 493). Shakespeare's uses of the word are concentrated in a trio of early works. He first used it twice in *Lucrece,* "spotted princess" (l. 172) and "her [Lucrece's soul's] sacred temple spotted," both times in relation to the soul. The word then appears in *Richard II* (3.2.134), "their spotted souls," an exact repetition of Southwell's usage, and in *A Midsummer Night's Dream* (1.1.110), "This spotted and inconstant man."[24] It seems very likely that Shakespeare picked the word up from Southwell and that he was struck by the idiosyncratic force of its moral and religious meaning.

Shakespeare seems also to have been impressed by Southwell's use of homely, even grotesque conceits, whose violence in their context is proportional to the mental distress being expressed or provoked. Southwell's stains-tears-water-washing-soaking imagery reappears in *Lucrece:*

> O that prone lust should stain so pure a bed,
> The spots whereof could weeping purify,
> Her tears should drop on them perpetually (ll. 684–86)

Here the words evoke both the staining of the bed linen and the moral defiling of the marriage, and as with Southwell's use of the imagery, the basis of the passage is the homely idea of stains that challenge the laundress's art. Shakespeare also has an image to rival Peter's steeped heart. When Colatine looks at his wife's ravaged face, "her eyes though sod in tears look'd red and raw" (l. 1592)—an even more grotesque version of Southwell's meat-in-water image. Peter's dried heart needed soaking; Lucrece's eyes are like soaked, or possibly boiled, meat. Shakespeare remained fond of the technique. Macbeth's description of the bloody daggers, "unmannerly breech'd with gore," which so offended Dr. Johnson, is a famous example. *Richard II,* close to *Lucrece* in date, style, and conception, has Richard's comparison of the flesh to a pie crust, "which serves as paste and cover to our bones" (3.2.154).

If one grants what seems to have been the case, that the appearance of Southwell's peculiarly intense, impassioned, and conceitist devotional style, in prose and verse, came as a revelation to contemporaries, then the relationship of *Lucrece* to the *Complaint* points to a milieu in which Southwell's work circulated among other writers. It also reveals something of the literary connoisseurship that the best Elizabethan writers brought to the reading of each other's work. Finally, it provides a literary context in which to read what is still one of Shakespeare's more difficult, puzzling works. Southwell's influence continued to resonate in Shakespeare's writing; *An Epistle of Comfort* underlies several passages in *King Lear.*[25]

Chapter Five

Southwell's Poetry: The Shorter Lyrics

The Canon

Except for the initials "R. S." on the title page of *Moeoniae* (1595), Southwell's publishers did not attribute his poems to him until the Jesuits of St. Omer produced their second edition in 1620. Nor is there any ascription of the poems to Southwell in the manuscript copies. In that context of silence, John Trussell's eagerness to blazon Southwell's name over his edition of *The Triumphs over Death* is all the more surprising. Nonetheless, despite the silence, Southwell's authorship of his various works was well known. A note among the Bacon papers identifies "Decease release" as "des vers de Mr. Southwell" (*Poems,* lxxvii), and Ben Jonson certainly knew who wrote "The burning babe" when he told Drummond of Hawthornden "that Southwell was hanged, yet so he had written that piece of his *The burning babe* he would have been content to destroy many of his."[1]

The three principal manuscripts (Stonyhurst A.v.27, Virtue and Cahill, British Library MS Additional 10422), each providing the same 52 poems in the same order, plus the poem "To the reader," fix the basic canon of Southwell's shorter pieces. In Nancy Pollard Brown's opinion, one of these poems, a clumsy translation of St. Thomas Aquinas's Corpus Christi hymn, "Lauda Sion salvatorem," may not be Southwell's. Brown included it in her edition "mainly out of respect for the compiler's judgment" (*Poems,* lxxviii). The Harmsworth Manuscript includes an additional 12 poems, of whose authenticity Brown is equally skeptical. The first two, "Conceptio B. Virginis sub porta aurea" and "Praesentatio B. Virginis," appear at the beginning of the manuscript and are meant to be part of a sequence on Mary and Jesus. The first of them is an earlier version of "The Virgin Mary's Conception," the first poem of the sequence. The two versions have the same riddling, witty third stanza, but one can see that the abstract grandeur of the Harmsworth version's first two stanzas, based on figures from the litanies of the Virgin, is not a suitable preparation for it:

> A golden gate was her conceiving place,
> That was the gate unto the golden age;
> The mine, the mint, the treasury of grace;
> Our gold to coin, and for to keep in gage,
> Wherewith the ransome of our sins was paid,
> Our pardon got, and all our debts defrayed. (*Poems,* 108)

"The Presentation of the Virgin," on the other hand, may well belong to the sequence, as Brown suggests, since the feast of the Presentation of the Virgin was reintroduced into the Roman calendar, 1 September 1585 (*Poems,* lxxxiii), and because the poem looks finished. The last of the additional poems is yet another version of a sequence poem, "The Annunciation altered from that before." Brown believes it is spurious, but without objective evidence, and there seems to be no strong reason not to believe that this is an early version too. Indeed, all these additions to the set of 52, except the sequence poem on the presentation of the Virgin, have the look of either early work or drafts. Three of them appear in *Moeoniae:* "The Virgin Mary to Christ on the cross," "Man to the wound in Christ's side," and "Upon the image of death." Their appearance in Busby's volume, printed from a different source (*Poems,* lxxxi) seems to guarantee their genuineness. There is also a four-stanza elegy for Lady Margaret Howard printed in *The Triumphs over Death,* and a stanza translated from Prudentius in *An Epistle of Comfort.* Including "The Author to the Reader" prefacing *Saint Peter's Complaint,* this makes a total of 70 short poems as printed in Brown's edition, not a large body of work.

The Nature of the Collection

As copied in the manuscripts, the poems' order reflects predominantly a grouping by theme and subject matter. First comes a sequence of 14 poems on the mysteries encoded in the mother-son relationship of Mary and Jesus. Then come four poems on the nativity and the Christ-child, followed by three on Christ's agony in the garden of Gethsemani. The next three poems belong to no grouping, and seem placed arbitrarily: "Joseph's amazement," a very peculiar and "incredibly bad" poem (Martz, 186) on Joseph's reaction to Mary's pregnancy; "An holy Hymn" (a translation of Aquinas's "Lauda Sion salvatorem"), and "Of the Blessed Sacrament of the Altar." A group of nine poems on sin occupies the central place in the collection. Although the central positioning of the group is not quite exact, it may be evidence of the design of Southwell's original collection. Then come eight poems on death or the wish to die, two on heaven in relation to the soul, and a final miscellaneous group of nine consisting of six gnomic poems and three persuasions against love, "Love's servile lot," "Lewd love is Loss," and "Love's garden grief."

Although the compiler made an attempt to group the poems according to kind or theme, no arrangement, however careful, can obscure the essentially miscellaneous character of the collection. Experience of reading it does not support Brown's belief that "the fifty-two lyrics have been arranged with sensitive awareness of the place of each in a framework of training in the spiritual life" (*Poems,* xcix). There is no particular reason why the last poems in the collection should conclude a training in the spiritual life, or why "Joseph's amazement" at Mary's pregnancy should come after the nativity poems, or be followed by two poems on the sacrament. Then there is the sheer disparity in the quality of the poems to be recognized; as materials for spiritual training, some are decidedly second-rate. It seems that not only the compiler, but Southwell himself, intent upon his program of literary conversion, failed to make some critical distinctions.

This failure of self-criticism, which in a writer as gifted as Southwell is really a failure of self-protection, even of self-esteem, may have been a consequence of his submission of himself and his faculties to his order and his mission. Warren Maurer, comparing Southwell to the German Jesuit poet Friedrich von Spee (1591–1635), produced a very interesting case parallel to Southwell's. Like Southwell, von Spee was of good family, was schooled in Continental humanism, was a missionary to his homeland, wrote a tract appealing for toleration, and left behind unpublished vernacular poetry whose similarity to Southwell's is due to "a very similar religious and literary environment": "The calculated intention to sermonize, combined with the burdensome need to sugar-coat the sermon to make it more palatable for the weak and fickle reader, all but stifles originality. The course often followed by our poets is to imitate popular profane models and render them morally harmless by turning them to the service of God. All too frequently, we see in their work the fabrications of literary craftsmen who, in their anxiety to hold the reader, stray from the path of inspiration."[2] Maurer agrees with Martz that the practice of meditation influenced sixteenth- and seventeenth-century poetry, but he suspects that in the case of the two Jesuits "their lifelong and rather regimented preoccupation with the art of meditation seems to have conditioned their creative powers along certain almost predictable lines" (16). And he adds that "it is hardly surprising that poetry written as an apostolic sideline should deal almost exclusively with God and things divine" (20).

This criticism has the accuracy of hostility. Joseph Scallon, who admires Southwell's poetry, also concludes that Southwell "began to compose verses on subjects which were dictated more by his zeal than by the concerns of his own spiritual life" (90). There is no doubt either, that Southwell had embarked on a campaign to convert contemporary secular love poetry to religious ends, and that it had unfortunate effects upon his poetic writing. This campaign was quite different from his other one for a new and original kind of religious literature, because its whole point was not to be original, but to appropriate others' writing for his own purposes. In many cases, he simply adopted a well-tried manner and preserved all its clichés, as in "S. Peter's remorse":

> Remorse upbraids my faults,
> Self blaming conscience cries,
> Sin claims the host of humbled thoughts,
> And streams of weeping eyes. (*Poems,* 33)

The worst that can be said about this conversion of a weeping Petrarchan lover to a weeping sinner is that as poetry it is boring, and, because bad literature never did anyone much good, as material for religious reading it would surely encourage smugness. Four of Southwell's poems express a wish to escape this sinful life by death ("Life is but Loss," "I die alive," "What joy to live," "Life's death, love's life"); in them Southwell has similarly converted the anthologies' Petrarchan lover who wishes to die into the sinful but repentant Christian who, while waiting for death and heaven, fills in the time by telling everyone how glad he will be to leave worldly love and transient beauty behind him (Janelle, 261–67).[3]

In a few cases, Southwell appropriated an actual poem for his sermonizing purposes. The most striking example is Sir Edward Dyer's "A Fancy." By deft substitutions, Southwell turns this graceful lament of a jilted lover (which is probably about Dyer's own loss of favor at Elizabeth I's court) into "a sinner's complaint." Martz, who admires the result, calls the process "parody" and relates it to Herbert's conversion of a love poem by the Earl of Pembroke (Martz, 189–91, 316) under the title "A parody." "Content and rich" (*Poems,* 67–69), another moralizing poem, is based on Dyer's "My mind to me a kingdom is"; "Love's garden grief," one of three persuasions against love, is probably based on Nicholas Breton's "A Strange Description of a Rare Garden Plot," published in *The Phoenix Nest* in 1593, but written much earlier (Thurston 1895, 239). Although neither of these poems is a line-by-line substitution of new text for old, Southwell's dependence on the originals is clear enough. "Love's garden grief," as Brown observes, is metrically experimental (lxxix), but apart from that it is an unpleasant poem, betraying an almost hysterical distrust of the natural body:

> Your coolest summer gales are scalding sighings,
> Your showers are tears,
> Your sweetest smell the stench of sinful living,
> Your favors fears,
> Your gardener Satan, all you reap is misery:
> Your gain remorse and loss of all felicity. (*Poems,* 64)

Martz's description of Southwell's appropriation of other poets' themes, style, and poems as "sacred parody" drew a sharp response from Rosamund Tuve. Martz (186n) claimed to be using "parody" in a neutral sense authorized by Herbert's use of the word as the title of his religious adaptation of a love poem by the Earl of Pembroke. Tuve responded by pointing out that all seventeenth-century definitions of the word "parody" "stress the element of mockery, burlesque, or at least some sidelong denigrating comment on the original author's sense," a meaning that does not fit Herbert's title at all, since Herbert is in no way mocking or caricaturing Pembroke's poem.[4] According to Tuve, there is no neutral meaning of "parody" in the period, and Martz was mistaken in trying to find one. If Herbert was following Southwell's "campaign to convert the poetry of profane love into the poetry of divine love" (Tuve, 252), then his use of "parody" is no more innocent or neutral than if he had written downright travesty. "No attitude toward another man's work is much less neutral than an intention to displace it entirely" (253)—a remark as acute as it is profoundly true.

The only meaning of parody that might help, Tuve argues, is the musical one: "replacement of text for a known tune," as well as the term *missa parodia* to describe masses using well-known tunes as thematic material. She then points out that serious "parodies" of this kind were not news in Southwell's or Herbert's time, and that they had been part of the great campaign of the Protestants—Luther, Marot, Bourgeois,

Coverdale, and the authors of *The Gude and Godlie Ballatis.* The reformers used "a musical practice to fulfill intentions they had as religious leaders: the intention does not inhere in the practice . . ." (259). To be fair to Southwell, providing words for music is probably exactly what he was doing: as he writes to his "loving cousin," "I send you these few ditties, add you the tunes" (Poems, 2). A ditty or song lyric provides the one notable success among his religious travesties of love poetry: "Marie Magdalen's complaint at Christ's death" can match any of the songs or "ditties" of the period for metrical skill and graceful statement:

> O my soul, what did unloose thee
> From thy sweet captivity?
> God, not I, did still possess thee:
> His, not mine, thy liberty.
> O, too happy thrall thou wert,
> When thy prison was his heart. (*Poems,* 46)

Thomas Morley recognized the quality of this poem by setting three of its stanzas to music in his *First Book of Ayres* (Martz, 192n). Another modest success owed to the writing of words for music seems to be "Man to the wound in Christ's side," a poem found in *Moeniae* and the Harmsworth manuscript, but not in the other manuscripts. The poem is an expansion of a petition in the prayer "Anima Christi," which precedes Ignatius's *Exercises:* "Within thy wounds hide me." It sounds more like an eighteenth-century evangelical hymn than an Elizabethan poem, and it illustrates C. S. Lewis's point that Southwell often seems to belong to no period:

> O pleasant port, O place of rest,
> O royal rift, O worthy wound,
> Come harbor me a weary guest,
> That in the world no ease have found. (*Poems,* 72)

Even so, and with all allowances made, Southwell's versified moral and religious commonplaces erected upon other poets' work add nothing to his poetic reputation. The same is true of the gnomic poems, a group that includes "Times go by turns," "Loss in delays," "Fortune's falsehood," "From Fortune's reach," and "Scorn not the least." It may be, as Brown suggests (lxxix), that these exercises in the style of the popular anthologies had a "hidden relevance" for the persecuted Catholics.

Christopher Devlin (180) makes a similar point about some lines from "Times go by turns," applying them to Southwell's own relief at a respite from persecution:

> Not always fall of leaf, nor ever spring,
> No endless night, yet not eternal day:
> The saddest birds a season find to sing,
> The roughest storm a calm may soon allay. (*Poems,* 58)

Nonetheless, the poetic temperature is low in all these poems, with the exception of the last of them, "Scorn not the least." The concluding couplets of these four six-line stanzas redeem them from the general dullness of the genre; they convey a sweet, rueful charm in which, at last, one may hear Southwell's own voice: "Yet higher powers must think, though they repine, / When sun is set: the little stars will shine."

The phrase "higher powers" is from Saint Paul's Epistle to the Romans, 13.1: "Let every soul be subject to higher powers," an injunction echoed by Southwell himself in his *Short Rule:* "Next my duty to God, it behooveth me to consider my duty to my superiors, whom I must account as his vicegerents and substitutes in the things wherein I am subject unto them" (*Letters,* 33). If for once there is a touch of wry humor in the use of the phrase in the poem, it is very acceptable.

These "second-hand" poems account for half of the collection. It is tempting to excuse the worst of them ("Joseph's amazement" or "The prodigal child's soul-wrack") as early work, even as exercises in English versification. We know that Southwell began writing about St. Peter and St. Mary Magdalen while he was in Rome, and so "Mary Magdalen's blush" might date from that time of his life. Most of these poems, though, probably date from his English years; Scallon (90) may well be right to suspect that Southwell simply allowed himself to be tempted into pious versifying for the good of the faithful. One thing is certain. Contemporary poets, such as Shakespeare, who admired *Saint Peter's Complaint,* would find nothing to interest them in these poems. Martz (184) thought that Southwell's attempt to convert love poetry to religious uses had influenced George Herbert, but there is nothing very specific about the parallels he adduces, and, as Tuve pointed out, there was nothing original about Southwell's activities. Even if there were, it would not improve the quality of the results, nor would it remove the taint of arrogant high-handedness attaching to the method. Plagiarism is not improved by being high-minded.

Southwell's poetic reputation rests upon the other half of the collection, which includes the 14 poems of the sequence on Mary and Jesus in six-line epigrammatic stanzas, the four nativity poems, the three Gethsemani poems, "A vale of tears," and two poems on heaven, "At home in heaven" and "Look home." All these poems except the last three are from the first part of the collection. Whether that means they were written first or last, or whether their position is merely coincidence, is something we shall never know.

The Sequence on Mary and Jesus

No external evidence survives to explain why this sequence exists, and no one has ever read it as a whole to find out how or why it is a sequence at all. Martz (101–7) speculated that it might be related to the devotion of the rosary, in particular to a version of it called "the *corona*" of Our Lady. Scallon responded to this suggestion by saying that "no-one has yet shown that there ever existed a form of the Rosary which included exactly those mysteries which Southwell has written about" (97). In Scallon's opinion, the poems are better considered as sacred epigrams, in the tradition of metaphysical and witty hymnody associated with Adam of St. Victor and Aquinas (100). Even so, one would like to know why Southwell wrote a sequence of them, and how many poems should be in it.

Because the publishers of the first collections broke the sequence up, Southwell's earliest readers did not know that the poems formed a sequence at all. Wolfe printed two of the poems, and Busby printed 10 more. The last two, "The death of Our Lady," and "The Assumption of Our Lady," omitted from the first English editions because they were too obviously Catholic, were not printed until 1856. If we include "The Presentation of the Blessed Virgin," preserved in the Harmsworth manuscript, the complete set would number 15 poems. Even with that poem added, there is a question whether the sequence forms a whole. If it is supposed to be on events in the joined lives of Mary and Jesus, why is there no poem on the deposition from the cross or on the miracle at Cana?

The first thing to be noticed about the sequence is that it is framed by poems on Mary's conception and birth, death and assumption; moreover, eight of the poems are about her as opposed to seven about Jesus. Since those are about his infancy and childhood, it seems clear enough that this is a Marian sequence, stressing the mystery as well as the motherhood of Mary—no reader of the printed text, however, could have known that until 1856. Indeed, Brown is the first editor to print the poems in the right order as a unit; and even she, because of her low opinion of the Harmsworth manuscript, omits "The Presentation of the Blessed Virgin," which has all the appearance of a complete, finished poem. Added to the set, that fifteenth poem determines the Marian bias of the whole, and equally important, provides the sequence with a center in the eighth poem on the circumcision.

The first poem, "The Virgin Mary's Conception," is in many ways characteristic of the set. There are three stanzas, each a completed statement in itself. The first imparts the mystery of the Immaculate Conception and its meaning:

> Our second *Eve* puts on her mortal shroud,
> Earth breeds a heaven, for God's new dwelling place,
> Now riseth up *Elias'* little cloud
> That growing shall distil the shower of grace:
> Her being now begins, who ere she end,
> Shall bring the good that shall our ill amend.
> ("The Virgin Mary's Conception," ll. 1–6)

The language is plain, the word order natural, and the form neat, yet the tone is mysterious and exalted. That Mary is a second Eve is a commonplace, but Southwell's mind is focused on the thought that if Eve has come again, the event means a new birth for the world, but a new death for her; she "puts on her mortal shroud." Even the common expression "puts on" acquires mystery in this context (as it does in Shakespeare's use of it, *Macbeth* (4.3.238–39): "The powers above / Put on their instruments"), first because it implies a decision to be conceived, and second because what is put on can be put off: this first line and its verb prefigure the end of the sequence with Mary's death and assumption. Meanwhile the earth that fell with our first Eve prepares to rise with the second, and in Mary it prepares a heaven for God to dwell in on earth. Mary, therefore, is already being spoken of as a microcosmic earth that contains a microcosmic heaven. The smaller contains the larger. Then, as the poem itself prefigures the whole sequence's end, so Southwell announces to us the mystery by which sacred history prefigured the Immaculate Conception as rain after drought in "Elias little cloud." The scriptural reference is to 3 Kings 18.42–45, where Elias (Elijah, *A.V.*) prays for rain, and instructs his servant to look towards the sea seven times: "And at the seventh time, behold a cloud arose out of the sea like a man's foot." The implication is that history, past, present, and future, is contained in this moment, which is therefore its microcosm. All that history, moreover, will be redeemed by the good that Mary will bring. The second and central stanza of the poem then spells out the central mystery of all: the making of this baby and this moment is the supreme work of grace and nature. "Both grace and nature did their force unite, / To make this babe the sum of all their best" ("Conception," ll. 7–8). As Brian Oxley first noticed, "A recurrent idea in Southwell's poetry is that of a place or person being a 'sum of beauty and delight'" (Oxley 1985b, 331). Here the phrase not only expresses Mary's microcosmic nature, but also looks forward to the end of the sequence when, in "The death of Our Lady," "the world doth lose the sum of all her bliss" (l. 2).

In this sequence, Southwell presents his reader with the idea that the world in which the Incarnation is the central event is a world of figures, correspondences, symmetries, antitheses, and paradoxes, all wrought by God as artificer in the medium of life through the agency of time, grace, and nature. Therefore, as if to amaze us with the curiosity, neatness, and sheer cleverness of the world's art, Southwell ends his poem with an ingenious last stanza:

> Four only wights bred without fault are named
> And all the rest conceived were in sin,
> Without both man and wife was *Adam* framed,
> Of man, but not of wife did *Eve* begin,
> Wife without touch of man Christ's mother was,
> Of man and wife this babe was bred in grace.
> ("The Virgin Mary's Conception," ll. 13–18)

If there is to be a quarternity of sinless beings in this world, then no two must come into it the same way: Southwell's God is not only an artist, but, like his poet, he is a mannerist artist, who enjoys being ingenious in detail.

Southwell's sources for these poems are the Bible, the patristic commentaries, and the liturgical texts (missal, breviary, hours and litanies of the Virgin). Enjoyment of the poems requires a taste for intricacy, wit, splendor, and exaltation—in a word, for the baroque. The elaborate art of the poems imitates the art of the cosmos they celebrate. The Bible may be the artist's book of plans and patterns, but the art itself engages just about every kind of art and craft. Here in three lines are tailor, quarryman, and architect:

For God on earth she is the royal throne,
The chosen cloth to make his mortal weed,
The quarry to cut out our corner stone. ("Her Nativity," ll. 13–15)

The cornerstone is Christ, as in Ephesians 2. 20: "Jesus Christ himself being the chief corner stone." God as architect has also made Mary, "A glorious temple wrought with secret art" ("Presentation of the Blessed Virgin," l. 1). Time, one of God's adjutants in the art of human history, is the learned chemist and physician who has extracted the significance from the words of the patriarchs and prophets, and applied it to our hurt souls:

The Patriarchs and Prophets were the flowers,
Which Time by course of ages did distil,
And culled into this little cloud the showers,
Whose gracious drops the world with joy shall fill,
Whose moisture suppleth every soul with grace,
And bringeth life to *Adam*'s dying race. ("Her Nativity," ll. 7–12)

The God who cures us is a surgeon: "The head is lanced to work the body's cure" ("His circumcision," l. 1), and a chemist: "The vein of life distilleth drops of grace" (l. 7). His angels prove to be connoisseurs: "Such dainty drops best fit their nectared cup" (l. 12). God is a gardener, too, who plants his tree of life in the paradise-garden he trusts to Joseph's care ("Her spousals"), and who transplants his flower from Egypt to Nazareth because Nazareth means "flower" ("Christ's return out of Egypt"). Even rhetorical, grammatical, and logical art has its place, expressing the mystery and surprise of life in puns, paradoxes, and antitheses: "Spell *Eva* back and *Ave* you shall find, / The first began, the last reversed our harms" ("The Virgin's salutation," ll. 1–2).

The artist of Southwell's cosmos has no objection to incongruity, either, and happily dresses himself in farm laborer's clothes in order to place a syllogism in a stable:

Man altered was by sin from man to beast:
Beast's food is hay, hay is all mortal flesh:
Now God is flesh, and lies in manger prest
As hay, the brutest sinner to refresh.
O happy field wherein this fodder grew,
Whose taste, doth us from beasts to men renew.
("The Nativity of Christ," ll. 19–24)

Above all, the art of Southwell's cosmos is an art of surprise, and of dramatic reversals: "Behold the father, is his daughter's son: / The bird that built the nest, is hatched therein" ("The Nativity of Christ," ll. 1–2). His art delights in disappointing normal expectation: "Man laboring to ascend procured our fall, / God yielding to descend cut off our thrall" ("The Virgin's salutation," ll. 17–18). Nor does it hesitate to work its transformations upon the most recalcitrant materials. There is even a place in its workshop for Herod's murdered babies to sing a silent song of blood to the accompaniment of tears and swords:

> O blessed babes, first flowers of Christian spring,
> Who though untimely cropped fair garlands frame,
> With open throats and silent mouths you sing
> His praise whom age permits you not to name,
> Your tunes are tears, your instruments are swords,
> Your ditty death, and blood in lieu of words.
> ("The flight into Egypt," ll. 13–18)

The cosmic artist's masterpiece of reversal and paradox is the crucifixion, the "good that shall our ill amend" prefigured in the first poem of the sequence. Centered in time and place, its centricity expressed in the form of the cross and in the figure of the body sacrificed upon it, Southwell has situated the crucifixion at the center of his sequence in the form of "His circumcision," a poem whose treatment of the circumcision as a type of the crucifixion is focused in the poem's central, third stanza:

> The vein of life distilleth drops of grace,
> Our rock gives issue to an heavenly spring,
> Tears from his eyes, blood runs from wounded place,
> Which showers to heaven of joy a harvest bring,
> This sacred dew let angels gather up,
> Such dainty drops best fit their nectared cup.

The blood and the water running into the cup prefigure the crucifixion and the mass. The water of the crucifixion that flowed from Christ's wound is the "shower of grace" foretold in "*Elias*' little cloud" and Moses' striking of the rock (Exodus 17.6). In the third stanza, the line "The knife that cut his flesh did pierce her heart" emphasizes the typology of the scene of the circumcision by its reference to the words of

Simeon to Mary, always taken as a prophecy of the crucifixion: "And thy own soul a sword shall pierce" (Luke 2.35).

Although Mary's role at the crucifixion is that of the watching, suffering mother, her role in this sequence devoted to her is to be the vessel in whom all this history is contained. She is the mother of human history, and when to human eyes she puts off her mortal shroud in death, she resumes her place with the immortal company of heaven. "The death of Our Lady" therefore begins, "Weep living things, of life the mother dies, / The world doth lose the sum of all her bliss"; "The Assumption of Our Lady" ends:

> Gem to her worth, spouse to her love ascends,
> Prince to her throne, queen to her heavenly king,
> Whose court with solemn pomp on her attends,
> And choirs of saints with greeting notes do sing.

The sequence therefore has a form and a subject. It is a celebration of Mary embodying in its own art ideas that profoundly moved and stimulated Southwell's imagination—above all his sense, as Oxley expresses it, "of the artifice of holy things, and indeed, of the holiness of artifice." "Rich and gorgeous" (Praz, 289) in its harmony of types, allegories, and paradoxes, but plain and elevated in language, the sequence is unique in English poetry. The irony of it, seen against the background of Southwell's dogged campaign to kidnap Tudor love poetry for the Church, is that in form and structure, the sequence is really Southwell's own love poem and its beloved is Mary as the "sum" of all human beauty and meaning. A conviction of the centrality of love was fundamental to Southwell's life, and first appears in his writing, before he was a professed Jesuit, in one of his Latin elegies, Elegia VIII. At the center (ll. 31–32) of this poem of 62 lines, in which a husband mourns his wife, are two of the most moving lines Southwell ever wrote:

> Dixi ego, ne dubita, memori vivemus amore,
> Quam tuus ipse tuus, tam mea semper eris.
> [I said, Doubt not, we shall live in the memory of love,
> As I am yours, truly yours, so you will always be mine.][5]

The reciprocity of love itself finds verbal form in these lines, in the paired words, in the effortlessly graceful movement of their language, in the interlinking of sounds (so that there is something like a pun on memori/amore), and in the antithesis that expresses the unity of "mine" and "thine." The same kind of writing appears in the sequence: "Her being now begins, who ere she end, / Shall bring the good that shall our ill amend," and "Our most, her least, our million, but her mite" ("The Virgin Mary's Conception," ll. 5–6, 9). Why, then, has so little attention been paid to the form and content of this sequence? Undoubtedly because until Brown published it almost intact for the first time in 1967, no one had seen it for nearly 400 years.

Sacred Epigrams: The Gethsemani Group and Others

Southwell's epigrammatic style appears again in three poems in six-line stanzas on Christ's agony in the garden of Gethsemani. They appear together in the manuscripts; Busby printed two of them, "Christ's bloody sweat" (omitting the second two stanzas) and "Christ's sleeping friends." The other, "Sin's heavy load," was first printed in Cawood's expanded edition of *Saint Peter's Complaint* (1602).

Martz thought that "Sin's heavy load" was one of the poems that revealed the influence of the Ignatian *Spiritual Exercises* on Southwell's poetics; the first two stanzas "suggest the acts of composition and memory, with a few touches of paradoxical analysis that prepare the way for the operations of the understanding" (Martz, 40–41). Yet the whole poem is a colloquy with Christ, and there is no sign of a "mental representation of the place" at all. In the second part of the poem, Southwell's control of his argument obviously slackens, a fault that has more to do with poetic form than with techniques of meditation. Brown, however, accepted Martz's suggestion, adding that the poem is "a meditation of the kind enjoined in the First Week of the Spiritual Exercises when the retreatant contemplates his own sin" (*Poems,* xcv). Most readers would probably agree with Martz that with its concentration on a single subject, and its argumentative, paradoxical approach, the entire poem foreshadows the methods of Donne.

The poem is based on verses found in the gospels according to St. Mark and St. Luke: "And when he was gone forward a little, he fell flat on the ground" (Mark 14.35); "And his sweat became as drops of blood, trickling down upon the ground" (Luke 22.44). Southwell incorporates the Douay-Rheims English texts into his first stanza with his usual accuracy, but what is really striking in this poem is that he puts himself into the stanza as the cause of Christ's fall:

> O Lord my sin doth over-charge thy brest,
> The poise thereof doth force thy knees to bow;
> Yea flat thou fallest with my faults oppressed,
> And bloody sweat runs trickling from thy brow:
> But had they not to earth thus pressed thee,
> Much more they would in hell have pestered me.

The essential paradox of the poem is that Christ, who holds the world in His hand, and supports the globe with a finger, is brought to the ground by the weight of one man's sin:

> O sin, how huge and heavy is thy weight,
> Thou weighest more than all the world beside,
> Of which when Christ had taken in his freight
> The poise thereof his flesh could not abide;
> Alas, if God himself sink under sin,
> What will become of man that dies therein?

In its best stanzas, then, the poem is really a strong, effective epigram based upon a conceit. It weakens in the fourth through sixth stanzas because Southwell departs from his original idea to develop the more elaborate conceit that, having fallen flat to earth at his arrival into Mary's womb, Christ now falls flat again in order to kiss the earth goodbye. This idea is too ingeniously pretty for the context, and might suggest to some readers that the first conceit is equally insubstantial, despite appearances. It is interesting, nonetheless, to see Southwell applying the charged, epigrammatic style of the sequence poems to other subjects.

The third poem, "Christ's sleeping friends," is a companion piece, similarly composed of seven six-line stanzas and based on the story of the apostles' falling asleep during Christ's agony. This time Southwell has avoided the excessive development of the first poem's conceit by devoting the first two stanzas to a plain narrative account of the disciples' sleep, and reserving the rest of the poem for the development of a single typological image based on the story of Jonas. He treats Jonas's sleep through the storm as a type of the disciples' carelessness, and the withering of Jonas's ivy tree as a type of the disciples' loss of Christ.[6]

The strength of both poems is in the powerfully emotive use of conceit and figure, which take on a life of their own, virtually independent of the thing figured. "Alas, if God himself sink under sin, / What will become of man that dies therein?" asks the speaker of "Sin's heavy load," having himself invented the conceit that it was his sins that made Christ fall in the first place. The speaker of "Christ's sleeping friends" addresses the disciples in the poem's last stanza as if they were learned in typological commentary, and were themselves become typological:

> Awake ye slumbering wights lift up your eyes,
> Mark *Judas* how to tear your root he strives,
> Alas the glory of your arbor dies,
> Arise and guard the comfort of your lives.
> No *Jonas'* ivy, no *Zacheus'* tree,
> Were to the world so great a loss as he.

The plain, energetic English suggests the presence of an author whose mind is on his subject, but his figure has so displaced the subject it was ostensibly introduced to explain that inevitably a reader will wonder exactly what the real subject of the stanza is. Is it a warning to people in a state of careless inattention, perhaps the less keen recusants? Is Christ himself figurative in this poem, standing for a threatened way of life? There is no way of knowing. What is clear is that the plain, narrative opening stanzas are in Southwell's plodding, Tottelian style ("From frighted flesh a bloody sweat did rain," l. 2), and that the language comes alive as it turns figurative. Southwell's most intricate figurative structures often seem to come untethered from the reality they should stand for, with the result that the poems can acquire an air of fantastic, ingenious abstraction.

The central poem of this set, "Christ's bloody sweat," a truly remarkable performance, is simultaneously a demonstration of the power and the danger of figurative language in Southwell's writing. Here there is no narrative exposition at all.[7] The translation of the event into figures begins immediately in the first stanza, an example of *carmen correlativum:*[8]

> Fat soil, full spring, sweet olive, grape of bliss,
> That yields, that streams, that pours, that dost distil,
> Untilled, undrawn, unstamped, untouched of press,
> Dear fruit, clear brooks, fair oil, sweet wine at will:
> Thus Christ unforced prevents in shedding blood
> The whips, the thorns, the nails, the spear, the blood.

The compiler of the Harmsworth manuscript wrote the first four lines in four columns, so that the reader immediately sees that the sentences read down as well as across. In this poem, the intense compression of the technique corresponds to the intensity and concentration of Christ's experience as a "prevention" or anticipatory experience of the Passion. The figures of soil, spring, olive, and grape contain compressed references to Old Testament texts interpreted as messianic prophecy, such as Isaias 12.3, "You shall draw waters with joy out of the saviour's fountains," and 63.2, "Why then is thy apparel red, and thy garments like theirs that tread in the winepress?" The bloody sweat is a compression of the entire Passion, summed in its instruments: whips, thorns, nails, spear, and cross. The root conception of the stanza seems to be the idea that Christ's agony was voluntary, and that by its very nature, it was also the kind of experience we call contemplative or mystical. Hence it will have come about, as the gospel narrative would suggest to a mind like Southwell's, by means of contemplative prayer. This first stanza therefore establishes a close parallel between the speaker and Christ. As Christ contemplated His own Passion in prayer, and proleptically entered into it through the realized figure of His own blood, so the poet contemplates Christ's Passion and prepares for his own figural embodiment of it. In that sense, the poem is the poet's equivalent of Christ's blood because it prays for and prefigures his martyrdom. There is, though, an important distinction to be made; although Christ's experience is a mystical one, similar to the Transfiguration, the poet's is not. He is the observer and imitator, not—as yet—the protagonist.

The second stanza is emblematic:

> He Pelican's, he Phoenix' fate doth prove,
> Whom flames consume, whom streams enforce to die,
> How burneth blood, how bleedeth burning love?
> Can one in flame and stream both bathe and fry?
> How could he join a Phoenix' fiery pains
> In fainting Pelican's still bleeding veins?

Southwell's fellow Jesuit, John Gerard, describes a crucifix decorated with the symbolism of phoenix and pelican (Gerard, 195). The phoenix, immolated in its own flames, is a symbol of resurrection, and the pelican, according to the bestiaries, revived its young by opening its own breast and feeding them its blood. Southwell treats both birds as examples of loving sacrifice, and the question he asks through the emblematic symbolism seems to be, how can one act combine two different sacrifices, the one motivated by a burning love and desire of a new life, the other by the wish to give oneself for others?

The answer comes in the third stanza with another shift in the mode of the poem, this time to Old Testament typology. In his contest with the priests of Baal (3 Kings 18.38), Elias produced a fire "that blood and wood and water did devour, / Yea stones and dust, beyond all nature's course" (ll. 15–16); the poet declares that "such fire is love." The last stanza is a prayer to that fiery divine love, and though the elaborate style has gone, the figures remain:

> O sacred Fire come show thy force on me
> That sacrifice to Christ I may return,
> If withered wood for fuel fittest be,
> If stones and dust, if flesh and blood will burn,
> I withered am and stony to all good,
> A sack of dust, a mass of flesh and blood.

This is no less than a prayer to be subsumed into figures, to have one's body transformed into a text of typological correspondences, and, of course, it is a preparatory contemplation of the nature of Southwell's own martyrdom. "Christ's bloody sweat" may be Southwell's finest poem, its tightly wrought web of figures finally enclosing the speaker inescapably in the determinist logic of typology. For that reason, it is also a terrible and tragic poem.[9]

Three other poems should be mentioned here. "Decease release: *dum morior orior,*" almost certainly about the beheading of Mary, Queen of Scots, on 8 February 1587, is the only accurately datable poem in the collection, and it shows Southwell as a master of his figurative, even riddling style quite soon after arriving in England—another hint that his career as an English poet had begun in Italy. The poem, spoken by the spirit of the dead queen, is another of his statements on martyrdom as a transforming sacrament: "God's spice I was and pounding was my due, / In fading breath my incense savored best" (ll. 5–6):

> Rue not my death, rejoice at my repose,
> It was no death to me but to my woe,
> The bud was opened to let out the rose,
> The chains unloosed to let the captive go. (ll. 25–28)

This poem in particular is notable for the strength and limpidity of its language, showing what the so-called plain, or "drab," style is capable of in the hands of a poet with as musical an ear as Southwell.

"At home in heaven" and "Look home" are a pair in the manuscripts. The first is about the love of God for the human soul, the second about the soul as a creature made for the love of God. They provide a glimpse of the kind of poet Southwell might have become had he lived a normal English life in his times. As Janelle remarked, the poems reveal a Platonic strain in their author. The soul of "At home" is in exile in this life, its beauty shrouded by veils of mortality; yet its beauty drew God down from heaven to become incarnate in human form: "Thy ghostly beauty offered force to God, / It chained him in the links of tender love." The link suggested between beauty and force, chains and tender love, has the ring of the metaphysical style in the mingling of extremely sensuous feeling and excited, even slightly kinky thought. Unfortunately, like most of Southwell's poems, this one has a didactic purpose—to dissuade its reader from earthly love—and after four superbly disciplined stanzas, it loses itself in prosy sermonizing. In the complementary poem, "Look home," Southwell writes that "Man's mind a mirror is of heavenly sights, / A brief wherein all marvels summed lie"; although the mind is a creature, it can also create, "To nature's patterns adding higher skill." This is possible because the mind is made in the image of God, Himself a craftsman "of endless skill and might."

Like "At home," "Look home" is not as benign as it looks at first. Its implication, spelled out Herbert-like in the title, is that since God made the soul to reflect himself, the sooner it turns its back to the world, the better.

The Nativity Group

The four poems on the nativity include Southwell's best-known lyrics, much anthologized. Benjamin Britten set words from two of them in his *Ceremony of Carols.* Part of the reason for their popularity is their simplicity. "New heaven, new war" is in six-line stanzas made up of octosyllabic couplets; "New prince, new pomp" and "The burning babe" are in ballad meter. "A child my choice" is in fourteeners, and though written in an elaborated syntax nonetheless gives an effect of simplicity:

> Alas, he weeps, he sighs, he pants, yet do his angels sing:
> Out of his tears, his sighs and throbs, doth bud a joyful spring.
> Almighty babe, whose tender arms can force all foes to fly:
> Correct my faults, protect my life, direct me when I die. (ll. 13–16)

Janelle, who argued that Southwell's writing developed from an over-elaborate, conceitist, and artificial style towards plainness and simplicity and who thought that the simpler poems were the later and better ones, praised "New prince, new pomp" for being "tender and plain," but criticized "The burning babe" for its hackneyed conceits (168). His predecessor, H. J. Thurston, also thought that Southwell's "affected style" was at odds with "the perfect earnestness and simplicity of Father Southwell's character" (Thurston 1895, 238), and naturally preferred the plainer poems. The taste of both these earlier critics, predating the modernist movement and its interest in the metaphysical style, was formed on different models from any that Robert Southwell knew. There is no reason at all to believe that in Southwell's mind a simple style was ever intrinsically better than a complex one. His nativity poems are probably more simply written for reasons of decorum; a plain ballad or carol-like style suits the subject of the nativity. Whether the poems were written earlier or later in his short poetic career is something we do not know.

In any case, simplicity of style does not necessitate simplicity of content. The first four stanzas of "New heaven, new war" summon the angels to leave home and follow their God's move to the stable on earth where He now is, and each angel is instructed to perform his traditional service there. The fiery seraphim who guard the ark of the covenant are invited to warm the Christ-child because the ark was one of His prefiguring types, and "This little ark no cover hath." Raphael, whose symbol is a fish, and who looked after Tobias, is asked to "provide our little Toby meat." Gabriel, who as angelic groom, "took up" the baby's first "earthly room" in Mary's womb, is to continue in the same employment. Michael the soldier is to guard him. The graces can rock him and all the other angels can sing his lullaby. The combination of angelology and typology with extremely simple, homely language is as clever as it is charming. The poem's fourth stanza announces to the angels the fundamental paradox of the nativity, that the baby in the manger is the God who made and sustains the cosmos or, as G. K. Chesterton expressed it, "The hands that made the sun and stars were too small to reach the huge heads of the cattle":[10]

> The same you saw in heavenly seat,
> Is he that now sucks Mary's teat;
> Agnize your King a mortal wight,
> His borrow weed lets not your sight.

With the second part of the poem, "new war," Southwell mobilizes another paradox, based on Matthew 10.34: "Do not think that I came to send peace upon earth: I came not to send peace, but the sword." The birth in the stable has opened a new front in the war against evil, mobilizing weakness against strength: "This little babe so few days old, / Has come to rifle Satan's fold"; that is, to plunder Satan's sheep-fold of its sheep. There follows a series of bold, even startling conceits:

> With tears he fights and wins the field,
> His naked breast stands for a shield;
> His battering shot are bab'ish cries,
> His arrows looks of weeping eyes,
> His martial ensigns cold and need,
> And feeble flesh his warrior's steed.

These conceits, a variant of St. Paul's instructions to the Ephesians to "put on the armour of God" (6.11), bring one very close to the basis and center of Southwell's own life and beliefs. The Christ child, as the God "Whom love hath linked to feeble sense" (l. 16), is the embodiment of life under the rule of love; and love, in the metaphysical warfare of the Christian soul with "principalities and powers, against the rulers of the world of this darkness,[11] against the spirits of wickedness in the high places" (Ephesians 6.12), is undefeatable because, according to a verse of one of Southwell's favorite biblical books, "Love is as strong as death" (Canticles 8.6). In the final stanza, Southwell addresses his own soul:

> My soul with Christ join thou in fight,
> Stick to the tents that he hath pight;
> Within his Crib is surest ward,
> This little Babe will be thy guard:
> If thou wilt foil thy foes with joy,
> Then flit not from this heavenly boy.

This apparently simple little poem, like *Saint Peter's Complaint* and "Christ's bloody sweat," is another version of Southwell's *imitatio Christi,* another stage in his contemplation of martyrdom. In form and content it belongs with his richest and most complex epigrammatic poems.

In its form at least, "New prince, new pomp" is a genuinely simple poem, carol-like in form and style. This is the poem that Martz used to demonstrate the presence of Ignatian meditative structures in sixteenth- and seventeenth-century poetry, the first two stanzas devoted to "composition, seeing the spot," the next four to "analytical acts of the understanding," and the last to arousing the affections to action in an exhortation (Martz, 39–40). An exhortation, however, is not the same as the colloquy with which a meditation is supposed to end and, furthermore, a meditation is a long and difficult form of prayer. This poem is very short and simple, and it is not a prayer. Its form could, nevertheless, reflect meditative technique; but if it does, then Ignatian meditation only formalized and schematized deeply ingrained mental habits in the service of Christian indoctrination. "New prince, new pomp" is typical of nativity carols and pageants in setting the scene, explaining it, and inviting the reader—or audience or congregation—to come and worship. As set by the English composer John Ireland, with a traditional "Nowell" for prelude,[12] it fits easily among other nativity carols such as the traditional Staffordshire carol, "The babe in Bethlehem's manger laid" (*Oxford Carols,* no. 69), or more modern examples such as Edward Caswall's "See amid the winter's snow"[13] and Christina Rossetti's "In the bleak midwinter" (*Oxford Carols,* no. 187).

No true nativity carol, however, can ever be intellectually simple; simplicity of form is always at odds with miraculous content, as in each of these three examples. The unsophisticated little Staffordshire carol almost takes the mystery for granted, but allows the angels their amazement at seeing God as a baby:

> The babe in Bethlehem's manger laid
> In humble form so low;
> By wondering angels is surveyed
> Through all his scenes of woe.

Christina Rossetti hints at the mystery ("A stable-place sufficed / The Lord God Almighty / Jesus Christ"), and Caswall spells it out: "Lo, within a manger lies / He who built the starry skies." In Southwell's case, the setting of the scene in its traditional detail is the prelude to the announcement of the mystery; in the baby shivering in a manger on a freezing winter night, the world is refigured according to His mother's own prophecy: "He hath put down the mighty from their seat, and hath exalted the humble" (Luke 1.52).

> This stable is a Prince's Court,
> The Crib his chair of state:
> The beasts are parcel of his pomp,
> The wooden dish his plate.
>
> The persons in that poor attire,
> His royal liveries wear,
> The Prince himself is come from heaven,
> This pomp is prized there.

The simple, humble style suits the occasion; the poem, one suspects, is Southwell's own gift to the child. Yet despite its simplicity, the miracle is fully acknowledged, and at the poem's turn from poor appearance to rich reality, the style rises to a tone of exalted conviction: "Weigh not his mother's poor attire, / Nor Joseph's simple weed. / This stable is a Prince's court. . . ."

The most famous of these poems, "The burning babe," combines the epigrammatic force of "New heaven, new war" with the carol-like simplicity of "New prince, new pomp" to produce a figure that has so far eluded all attempts to explain it. Standing shivering in the snow on a frosty winter's night, the poet feels a sudden warmth that makes his heart glow. Looking up to see where the fire might be, he sees in the air a burning, weeping baby, who speaks to him, explaining what he is. The explanation complete, the baby vanishes, "And straight I called unto mind, / That it was Christmas day."

Janelle (168) said of the poem that "despite its prettiness and sweetness, [it] contains the most hackneyed of all conceits" in the lines on the baby's tears and flames—a view that, besides leaving the poem unexplained, disposed of its central mystery entirely. More recently, it has been suggested that the image of the burning baby derives mostly from the emblem book tradition, where such images as flaming hearts, fiery hearts in furnaces, and fountains pouring blood are to be found.[14] Unfortunately, although the baby certainly explains himself as if he were familiar with emblem book practice, no emblem of a burning baby has been found. In any case, Southwell's baby does not behave like an emblem. Another scholar has suggested that the image of the burning babe derives from a typological reading of the burning bush as prefiguring the Virgin and the Incarnation, with an implication that Queen Elizabeth is a new pharaoh, Southwell a new Moses.[15] A burning bush, however, is not a burning baby; it may be an analogue, but it is not a precedent. Martz produced passages from the *Meditations* of Luis Puente on the fire of love in Jesus' heart as context for his argument that this poem, too, was the product of Ignatian meditation, "an application of the senses" following upon a meditation, and beginning with "a particularly vivid 'composition'" (Martz, 81–82). Martz is almost certainly right in thinking that the poem is the result of meditation, even if the technical language is out of place. For instance, the poem does not begin with a "composition" or "mental representation of the place"; it begins with a vision, and ends with its disappearance. John R. Roberts, who accepts Martz's view of the influence of the *Spiritual Exercises,* believes that the poem records a mystical experience: "There is a note here of his having lost himself in ecstatic delight, the goal of Ignatian methodology,"[16] a view with which Geoffrey Hill disagrees: "For Southwell to have 'lost himself' merely in a poem would have required more self-centredness than he was capable of" (Hill, 36).

Practice of the Ignatian exercises could lead to mystical experience, but that was not their purpose, which was instead to discipline and indoctrinate the retreatant. If the experience in "The burning babe" were the poet's, he would have undergone a physical phenomenon well-known to adepts in mysticism as the incendium amoris, or fire of love, which was by no means uncommon in the fervent atmosphere of Counter-Reformation Catholicism. Saints Philip Neri, Catherine of Genoa, Stanlislaus Kostka, and Veronica Giuliani all claimed to experience it. It was a sensation of intense heat in and about the heart, which St. Veronica Giuliani is said to have experienced to the extent of being "stigmatized" with a curved right shoulder. A surgeon's affidavit of 1673 from Naples claims that an autopsy upon a nun, Sister Maria Villani, revealed "smoke and heat which exhaled from the heart, that veritable furnace of love." The surgeon even burned himself on the heart, in which he found a wound "made with a spear of fire."[17]

Southwell would have known of this phenomenon, just as he was familiar with the devotional language of blood, wounds, hearts, and flames. The baby of the poem certainly seems to be experiencing "the fire of love." Southwell uses English precisely, and as Geoffrey Hill observes, the baby's "excessive heat" (l. 9) means heat accompanying, or associated with, "excess," used in the Latin sense of "being outside oneself," in "ecstasy."[18] The poet, standing in the heat radiating from the baby, feels his heart glow—but that is all. Indeed, in the structure of its thought, this poem is similar to "Christ's bloody sweat." In both poems Christ, here the burning Christ-child, undergoes the experience: the poet observes it. The implication is that the poet must imitate it, first in his poem, then in his life.

At the poem's center is a vision of the mystery of divine love as it is expressed in the gospel of St. John, 3.16: "For God so loved the world, as to give his only begotten Son; that whosoever believeth in him, may not perish, but may have life everlasting"; and once again Southwell presents God as an artist or craftsman, this time working his transformations in metal:

> My faultless breast the furnace is,
> The fuel wounding thorns:[19]
> Love is the fire, and sighs the smoke,
> The ashes, shame and scorns;
>
> The fuel Justice layeth on,
> And Mercy blows the coals,
> The metal in this furnace wrought,
> Are mens' defiled souls.

The lines resist close paraphrase, but one gathers that justice or law fuels the fire of divine love with man's cruelty and inhumanity, and that mercy or compassion intensifies the fire as it smelts and refines the impurities out of souls: the Christian who imitates this Christ will have to go into some very dark corners of the human scene indeed.

How is a reader to understand the factual, expository opening and close of the poem? We know from the prefatory material to *Mary Magdalen's Funeral Tears* that Southwell did not care for fictions, and so we should probably allow that in some sense, if only in his mind's eye, Southwell saw this baby on Christmas night. For him, the stable of the nativity, usually imagined as a scene of peace and joy, prefigured the Passion of Christ and the martyrdom of His disciples. Helen White, who distinguished between the "discursive development of the meditative" and "the total-working immediacy of the contemplative" thought that "The burning babe" was a truly contemplative poem.[20]

"A Vale of Tears"

For twentieth-century readers, the most impressive of Southwell's short poems is probably "A vale of tears," a 19-stanza *paysage moralisé* of the troubled mind quite unlike anything else to be found in Elizabethan poetry. It is based (like a famous passage of Byron's *Journal to Augusta*[21]) on Southwell's own experience of crossing the Alps twice, on his way to and from Italy. "The poem most likely reveals the deep impression produced upon him by the wild, majestic and weird scenery in the neighbourhood of the St. Gothard pass" (Janelle, 278). Janelle is surely right; indeed, the first thing to strike one about the poem's form is its composed objectivity, as if the scene had been "photographed" by the poet's memory. The first two stanzas fix its outlines visually, and the attention paid to the movement of the eye in comprehending the scene is especially interesting:

> A vale there is enwrapped with dreadful shades,
> Which thick of mourning pines shrouds from the sun,
> Where hanging clifts yield short and dumpish glades,
> And snowy flood with broken streams doth run,
>
> Where eye-room is from rocks to cloudy sky,
> From thence to dales with stony ruins strowed,
> Then to the crushed water's frothy fry,
> Which tumbleth from the tops where snow is thowed.

The next three stanzas supply the sounds of this enormous, but enclosed place, "Where ears of other sound can have no choice" but wind, water, and thunder: "And in the horror of this fearful choir, / Consists the music of this doleful place."

Having provided a general picture of the valley, Southwell then spends four stanzas on the response of travelers to it. No-one goes there, he says, but pilgrims—people like himself, that is, going to and from Rome. The valley terrifies them, and "They judge the place to terror framed by art"; but they are wrong: "Yet nature's work it is of art untouched, . . . / A place for mated minds," that is, for the terrified and helpless. Four stanzas of detail follow:

> Huge massie stones that hang by tickle stay,
> Still threaten fall, and seem to hang in fear,

> Some withered trees ashamed of their decay,
> Beset with green, are forced gray coats to wear.

This part of the poem closes with a pair of stanzas announcing that this valley, "Where sorrow springs from water, stone and tree," is a place for "pangs and heavy passions," and for "plaining thoughts."

Only in the last four stanzas, in an address to his own soul, does the poet relate the landscape to himself. For him it is a place for tears and repentance, and it becomes clear when he says "Set here my soul main streams of tears afloat" that "here" can only be a mental place, and that this is a mental landscape. Is Martz right, then, to argue that "This is no romantic landscape" but an allegorical setting for a meditation; specifically, that it represents the two "preludes" for the meditation upon one's sins (Martz, 207–8)? In this as in other poems, Southwell may have been influenced by his Jesuit training, but no objective evidence exists anywhere that Southwell made poems out of meditations. To use the word "romantic" to dispose of the contrary view sets up a straw man; no one would mistake this poem for a work of the romantic period. On the other hand, most readers have seen some preromantic tendencies in it, not only in the detailed evocation of a wild alpine landscape and the projection of unhappy states of mind onto it, but in Southwell's aesthetic description of the place, with its "disordered order" and "pleasing horror." Few readers will wish to confine so original a poem within the form and purpose of Jesuit meditation.

In this connection, the most interesting feature of the poem is its musical imagery, which appears in the first stanza in the phrase "dumpish glades," a "dump" being a sad piece of music as well as a generally sad state of mind. The sounds of wind, water, and thunder make the "music of the place"; the pleasant songbirds have left it, and only heavy notes have any "grace"—a musical term meaning ornament. The phrase "disordered order" is an invitation to think of a certain kind of chromatic music, greatly favored in Southwell's time to express melancholy and distress. Music is mentioned in all the last four stanzas addressed to the poet's soul. In the first, the ditties, or words, are to be set to solemn tunes in the saddest kind of music, and in the second, "*Echo,*" a common imitative effect in music, will repeat "thy plainful cries." "Dumps" return in the third of these stanzas, and in the last, tears are to be set to tunes and pains to plaints, and the whole acquires a burden or refrain: "Come deep remorse, possess my sinful brest: / Delights adieu, I harbored you too long."

In a context of so much intensely musical imagery, the line "Set here my soul main streams of tears afloat" also becomes musical, the phrase "streams of tears" evoking a musical composition that, if ever realized, would have been akin to the best-known song of the period—also popular in instrumental form—the *lacrimae,* or "tears," of the great recusant lutenist, John Dowland.[22] Dowland, born in 1563, was almost exactly contemporary with Robert Southwell. "A vale of tears" is a text for an expressive musical setting; the poem is full of invitations to musical word-painting on the part of a composer:

> A place for mated minds, an only bower,
> Where every thing doth sooth a dumpish mood.
> Earth lies forlorn, the cloudy sky doth lower,
> The wind here weeps, here sighs, here cries aloud.

This being so, the text transcends any origin some elements of its form might have had in meditative habits, or in Southwell's campaign to convert secular verse. The burden, "Delights adieu, I harbored you too long," places the poem firmly in a social context, however pious. Its speaking voice is not necessarily Robert Southwell's, but the voice of its singer, and for that reason the poem almost certainly exceeds in significance any intention Southwell himself might have had for it. As a distinguished musicological critic has written of this kind of introspective composition for words and music, "The Elizabethan's delight in the wonders of the physical universe is explicitly related to his preoccupation with his own mind and senses. Exploring nature and exploring the self are the same activity, *both opposed to antique theological dogma*" (my italics).[23] Southwell probably intended his poem to be another encouragement to repentance for sin, but the nature of the landscape and the range of responses possible to it engulf the intention. There is no better evidence of the strength and originality of Southwell's poetic gift than this strikingly forward-looking, even prophetic poem.

Chapter Six
Southwell Then and Now

Saint Peter's Complaint and Southwell's shorter poems began to circulate in manuscript before his death, probably even before his arrest. Thus, quite apart from the fame caused by his death, there was an audience for his work in 1595, and from the day of publication *Saint Peter's Complaint* was a popular book. It went into fifteen editions by 1636, which puts it in the same best-seller class as Shakespeare's *Venus and Adonis,* of which there were 15 editions by 1640. (There were eight editions of *The Rape of Lucrece* in the same period.) *Mary Magdalen's Funeral Tears* was also popular, with eight editions by 1636. Although Nancy Pollard Brown attributed the drying up of the stream of editions to growing Puritan influence (*Poems,* lxxvi), the decline of interest in Southwell also coincided with a major shift in taste from the conceitist style to a poetics of nature, civility, and good sense—a shift signaled by the publication of Milton's poems in 1645. Interest in Shakespeare's narrative poems waned at about the same time, and no doubt for the same reason.

Brown believes that the only explanation for the great popularity of Southwell's volume of poems is that *Saint Peter's Complaint* versified Catholic teaching on the sacrament of penance (Brown 1966, 3). Certainly, many people must have read Southwell with pious motives; he created a considerable market for the literature of tears and repentance, as the many imitations of his books suggest, nearly all of them by negligible writers.[1] Alongside the evidence of pious interest, however, are signs of Southwell's influence on serious writers. Shakespeare's *Lucrece* and Drayton's *Matilda the Fair,* both published in 1594 and probably written in 1593, provide evidence that their authors had read *Saint Peter's Complaint.*[2] Gabriel Harvey, who praised the *Funeral Tears* for being "elegantly and pathetically written," taunted Nashe with his plagiarism of the book: "Now he hath a little mused upon *The Funeral Tears of Mary Magdalen,* and is egged on to try the suppleness of his pathetical vein." Devlin has argued that Nashe knew the *Epistle of Comfort,* too. Francis Bacon was so impressed by the style of *An Humble Supplication,* though not its argument, that he sent the manuscript (which Topcliffe had lent him) to his brother for copying (Devlin, 266, 254). Ben Jonson's praise of "The burning babe" has already been quoted. A conviction that Herbert knew Southwell's poetry, and was indebted to it, is fundamental to Louis Martz's *Poetry of Meditation.*

John Bodenham's *Belvedere, or The Garden of the Muses* (1602) provides evidence of Southwell's appeal for the ordinary reader of poetry.[3] This large collection of quotations from contemporary poets is a rough guide to the fame and popularity of the poets represented. Drayton has the largest number of quotations in the book (269), followed by Spenser (215), Shakespeare (214), and Lodge (79). Southwell shares the fifth place with Daniel; both are represented by 75 quotations.[4] In Southwell's case the quotations are all from the two small books, *Saint Peter's Complaint* and *Moeoniae,* whereas the quotations from the other authors are drawn in each case from a much larger body of work. The mere number of Southwell quotations, therefore, doesn't fairly represent his place. Bodenham's collection was meant for a discriminating readership, and at least one such reader, Edmund Bolton, left a concise summary of the qualities that drew people to read Southwell: "Never must be forgotten *Saint Peter's Complaint,* and those other serious poems said to be Father Southwell's; the English whereof, as it is most proper, so the sharpness and light of wit is very rare in them" (cited by Hood, 76).

In its own time, and for a generation afterwards, Southwell's writing appealed to a wide readership, encompassing the pious, the poets, and the ordinary literate reader. With the passing of the taste for that highly ornamented, conceited style, Southwell and his writings dropped out of sight for the larger audience and retained only a small audience of coreligionists who valued the record of his life and martyrdom over his writing. Robert Southey knew Southwell's poems, and valued them enough to encourage W. Joseph Walter to publish his edition of *Saint Peter's Complaint and Other Poems* in 1817,[5] but otherwise there is little sign of any general interest until Quiller-Couch included "Of the Blessed Sacrament of the Altar" and "The burning babe" in *The Oxford Book of English Verse* (1900). In fact Southwell's style was an embarrassment to Catholic readers. Herbert Thurston, after pointing out that Southwell was one of the most popular writers of his time, added that that was not necessarily evidence of literary merit (Thurston 1895, 231). Christobel M. Hood prefaces her selection of poems with an apology: "The heavily ornamented style which so pleased his contemporaries is tedious to readers in the twentieth century," and although she exempts the poetry from this criticism, she says that "the imagery and style" of *Saint Peter's Complaint* "are often too fantastic to please modern taste" (Hood, 70, 73–74). Janelle, too, dislikes the ornamented style, and makes Southwell's development from an elaborate to a plain style into the thesis of his book. The fundamental criticism being made by these readers is that Southwell's complex style obscures the real, natural Southwell, whom they see as a man of great simplicity and charm. Therefore, the style must be a disguise of some kind adopted as a compromise with the fashions of the age in order to carry on the work of the mission. Even his modern editor adopts this utilitarian view of Southwell as a writer. Not until 1985, in what are probably the two most important critical articles on Southwell, did Brian Oxley spell out what should have been clear all along: "Artifice is central to Southwell's poetry, his conception of religion, and his life" (Oxley 1985b, 330).

Modern scholarly criticism has taken a different approach, determined largely by Louis Martz's ground-breaking study, *The Poetry of Meditation.* In this book, Martz undertook a bold and difficult task: to show that this minor, neglected Jesuit writer was the source of the mainstream of English seventeenth-century lyrical poetry. The method was to give an account of the art of meditation, treating Ignatius Loyola's *Spiritual Exercises* as the key document for the sixteenth century, and then, after explaining and demonstrating meditative form, to show how it is replicated in poetry, beginning with three of Southwell's poems. Martz's subject matter was entirely new for most of his scholarly readers, and his thesis made a strong impression. Most of the scholarship on Southwell since Martz begins by accepting his thesis, and either refining upon it or else developing a special corner of it—by offering to show, for example, the sources of his imagery.

Martz's book had two weaknesses, one general, the other particular. First, the book tries to prove its thesis by comparing meditational form to poems. There is no actual evidence that the poets read or followed these religious texts, except, of course, for Southwell, who was a professional. But even in his case there is no evidence that he consciously set out to write "meditative" poetry. The comparative method in this case is faulty because, as Joseph D. Scallon insists in his study of Southwell, poetry and prayer are different things, and remain so even though "it seems natural to suppose that the habits of thought formed by [Ignatian meditation] carried over into his poetic composition" (Scallon, 89). Because Martz's method passes over Scallon's distinction, it obscures some essential critical questions, namely, how does a poet *meditate* a poem into existence, and how does he approach the question of style? It cannot be a question of simply looking into the heart and writing. As

Scallon says, "There is no evidence that Southwell ever experienced any of the extraordinary forms of prayer described by Teresa of Avila or John of the Cross" (90). For him, all is art and composition. Moreover, when one reflects that affective devotion is at the heart of Counter-Reformation piety, and that it influences all forms of religious art and worship, it seems likely that Ignatian meditation was a manifestation rather than a cause of a development that occurred more or less simultaneously in various fields of European activity. In Southwell's case, his training as Jesuit would have systematized tendencies already present in him as a poet and writer.

Second, as a study of Southwell, Martz's book suffers from its treatment of him as the forerunner, the influencer, the experimenter. By the time Martz comes to give an overview of Southwell's career, the most interesting poems have already been discussed—in each case as an example of something else, not as a poem in itself. Because the *Short Rule of Good Life* is related to the other devotional treatises, and because Martz can relate *Mary Magdalen's Funeral Tears* to the meditative style, he discusses both at length; but the *Epistle of Comfort, The Triumphs over Death,* and the *Humble Supplication* receive no mention. Consequently, an entire zone of Southwell's writing is missing from the picture, and fundamental questions of style and intent are not raised. Martz's book remains an important contribution to knowledge of the intellectual and devotional contexts of seventeenth-century verse, but it introduced Robert Southwell to mainstream historical criticism as the exponent of a specialized, even exotic branch of English literature. This became clear when sixteenth-century sectarianism surfaced again, however politely, in Barbara Kiefer Lewalski's *Protestant Poetics.* Lewaski argued vigorously against Martz's thesis, and denied Southwell any role at all in the making of seventeenth-century English lyric poetry, presumably on the eminently logical premise that a Catholic could not have influenced Protestant poetics. Southwell's contemporaries took a less stringent view of the workings of influence.

Where then do we place this martyred Jesuit whose poems and prose writings reached as wide and varied an audience as Shakespeare's poems? The question has no easy reply. One can begin by agreeing with C. S. Lewis that Southwell is an individual figure. He belongs to no school, and in all likelihood begot none either, despite his influence on contemporaries. Southwell's isolation, however, has nothing to do with personal individuality or eccentricity; rather it is the problematic isolation of a man who has chosen to oppose himself to his world. Lewis's assessment of the poetry is probably fair, too, taken simply as description: "Southwell's work is too small and too little varied for greatness: but it is very choice, very winning, and highly original" (Lewis, 546). Yet the judgment is based on assumptions Southwell never made; he never aimed at Lewis's kind of range or greatness. On the contrary, by being what he was in his England, he chose what to others was narrowness, but to him was everything. In general, of course, his theme was his religion; but the single, fundamental theme of Southwell's most characteristic writing is sacrifice motivated by love. It appears as much in the graceful, even naive-sounding simplicity of the Christmas poems as in the baroque complexities of "Christ's bloody sweat." It is the prime motive of his Mary Magdalen, and the supreme gift offered to his fellow Catholics in *An Epistle of Comfort.* His St. Peter is ashamed because he has betrayed his love to save himself. The theme of Southwell's writing was also the theme of his life; from the moment he entered the Jesuit novitiate he prepared himself for the ultimate sacrifice of martyrdom. Southwell not only wrote about sacrifice; he wrote himself as sacrifice and lived what he had written. As Oxley writes, "Southwell's art aspires to imitate the heavenly composition of God" (Oxley 1985b, 340), and there seems to have been no doubt in Southwell's mind that God's transforming masterpiece was the Passion, which, in reclaiming humanity, remade history. When Robert Southwell stood in his shirt on a cold February day waiting to be hanged, he was on the threshold of achieving his own life's masterpiece and ambition.

What can literary history make of such a figure? One can no more separate Southwell's life and writing than Byron's, and the challenge to preconception offered by Southwell's career is nicely expressed in the title of Geoffrey Hill's essay: "The Absolute Reasonableness of Robert Southwell." For Hill, "the most crucial of confrontations, the most searching of contexts" is provided by one of Southwell's interrogations before the Privy Council, at which he was complimented on his courtesy and asked why he had not spoken equally reasonably to Topcliffe. "Because," Southwell answered, "I have found *by experience* that the man is not open to reason" (Devlin, 287, citing Hill, 26). As Hill goes on to say, in the experience of men like Southwell normal reason "was compromised at every turn by 'reason of state.' Southwell's retort, in an instant, judges the travesty and redeems the word" (26). A little later in the essay, Hill finds a "paradigm" for Southwell's "absolute reason" in a passage of St. Cyprian, quoted in *An Epistle of Comfort:* "Why dost thou turn thee to the frailty of our bodies? Why strivest thou with the weakness of our flesh? Encounter with the force of our mind; impugn the stoutness of our reasonable portion; disprove our faith; overcome us by disputation if thou canst, overcome us by reason (205a). "Force of mind" in Southwell's case, writes Hill, "is manifested in the power to remain unseduced and unterrified" (34).

To say that Southwell was never seduced or terrified would be an exaggeration. He certainly knew terror, as the letter written "from the threshold of death" on the eve of sailing to England shows, and he had his moments of being seduced by the intellectual and linguistic violence of his age. Writing in Latin, in the 12 letters discovered in Rome by Philip Caraman, all but two dating from the first 30 months of his mission, Southwell could be surprisingly brutal. On 12 August 1587, describing the burning of a Protestant heretic in Norwich, he calls the relics of the victim (which disappeared from the site) "faeces"; "crap" would be an apt modern synonym. Early in 1588, in a long, jeering passage, he describes William Whitaker, Regius Professor of Divinity at Cambridge, as a well-known maker of lies and a "miles gloriosus," the braggart captain of Plautine comedy. Southwell's report of Leicester's death, in a letter of 7 September 1588, is the conventional party vituperation of his period; Leicester is an abstract of wickedness, a glutton for crimes, who left no sin uncommitted, and who has made a spectacular entrance into hell.[6]

The presence of commonplace vituperation in these early letters renders the achievement of the prose of the *Humble Supplication* all the more impressive. One doubts whether the young Southwell, having compared the loyalty of Catholics and Puritans to the disadvantage of the latter, could have gone on to write, "We speak not this to incense your Majesty against others, being too well acquainted with the smart of our own punishments to wish any Christians to be partakers of our pains" (*Supplication,* 27). The key word there is "Christians," a word not readily used of each other by religious opponents in Southwell's time. Such a sentence vindicates Geoffrey Hill's statement that in all cases, but especially in Southwell's, style is a question not only of what one says, but also of what one chooses not to say (Hill, 27). In that one sentence of the *Supplication* one can see the principle of transformative imitation that animated Southwell's life penetrating and shaping his style. In doing violence—to use his own scriptural locution—to his own anger and violence, he seems to have renounced the violence of his age in all its forms, including the literary violence of controversy.

Sacrifice and renunciation produced in Southwell a uniquely isolated, lonely figure who, despite popularity and influence could never be accepted as part of a way of life and a tradition he rejected so uncompromisingly, even fanatically, in all its forms. One might be tempted to argue that he retained at least an aristocratic pride of birth and breeding; but the letter to his father makes it plain that considerations of family took second place to his religious zeal. Besides, there could be no more complete a renunciation of social honor than death by hanging. Renunciation is a continual theme in his writing. "For while we live, we die, and then we leave dying, when we leave living. Better therefore it is to die to life, than to live to death" (*Epistle,* 117a–b). The belief that life is death and that death is victory brought Southwell the martyr's freedom from every allegiance and, by implication, the freedom of indictment as well. It enabled him to remain silent under torture, thus indicting his government of illegal, barbarous, and stupidly wicked behavior. At his execution, it enabled him to cast the government in the Herodian role of antichrist. Linked as it must be with his poetics, Southwell's freedom also indicted his literary culture for its complicity in the violence and falsehood of the time; and by the Southwellian standard the indictment presumably extends to what we call English literary tradition—or Protestant poetics, to coin a term—entwined as it is with the violent and sometimes savage history of the English people in the sixteenth and seventeenth centuries.

At the very least, the implications of a career such as Southwell's are discomfiting to complacency about English history and tradition, and at least one important contemporary seems to have been as discomfited by Southwell's performance as any twentieth-century reader could be. John Donne, who grew up in the very center of English Catholic loyalism, and who certainly knew about Southwell and may well have met him, wrote his long, densely argued book *Pseudo-Martyr* against the conception of the Church that Southwell submitted himself to and died for. Insofar as Southwell's martyrdom or act of witness was a statement made against his nation, *Pseudo-Martyr* was meant to be a rebuttal of it. Donne argues that there are three grounds on which to claim martyrdom: "The first is, to seal with our blood the profession of some *moral Truth,* which though it be not directly of the body of the Christian faith, nor expressed in the *Articles* thereof, yet it is some of those works, which a Christian man is bound to do. The second is, to have maintained with loss of life, the *Integrity* of the Christian faith, and not to suffer any part thereof to perish or corrupt. The third is, to endeavor by the same means to preserve the *liberties* and *immunities* of the Church."[7] The third ground would seem to provide for Southwell's case, especially since, as Donne explains, the Church's liberties and immunities are of two kinds, "native" and "accessory." The first kind include "preaching the word, administering the sacraments, and applying the Medicinal censures," and the second kind are those established "for the furtherance and advancement of the worship of God" by "Christian Princes." Anyone who dies for carrying out the first kind, or even for "a dutiful and pious admonition to the Prince" to maintain the second kind, is a martyr (Donne, 154). For Donne, however, writing as a Protestant in a country that denied martyrdom on precisely those grounds to Saint Thomas of Canterbury,[8] Donne's third ground could not validate martyrdom in the case of Southwell and his fellow Catholics.

Like other controversialists of his time, Donne marshalls a complex and difficult argument to maintain a simple, predetermined point, which he states bluntly in his "Preface to the Priests and Jesuits": "It is not the Catholic faith, which you smart for, but an unjust usurpation" (*Pseudo-Martyr,* 23)—by which he means the claims of the Papacy, and specifically the claim to temporal power over princes. As is virtually always the case in these controversies, Donne's argument is the mirror image of his opponents'; whereas they ground the Church's institutional life upon the rock and chair of Peter, he grounds it upon the secular power of the prince. As his editor explains, Donne's argument is a subtle one, which goes rather like this: historically, the secular state precedes the spiritual state; by typology and analogy the revelations of scripture transform the secular state into a state both secular and spiritual, whose ruler, like David or Solomon, or King James I of England, can combine in himself spiritual and secular functions. Donne then argues that what can be combined can be separated. Every native-born subject of the Crown owes allegiance to it because the secular authority is fundamental to the state; the spiritual authority, on the other hand, is donated, and is not similarly binding. Therefore Donne "argued with English Catholics in *Pseudo-Martyr* that it was quite thinkable for them to swear allegiance to their Protestant king . . . and yet also swear loyalty to the spiritual ruler of another state like Paul V" (*Pseudo-Martyr,* l). Hence, a man like Southwell forfeits all right to the title of martyr because he has refused to defend his life by a perfectly lawful action, namely taking the oath of allegiance (154–55), and renouncing the temporal authority of the Pope in England. Pursued to its logical conclusion, Donne's argument would make Southwell into a suicide.

Donne's view, shorn of its scholastic and humanist apparatus of argument, has prevailed in English history, which has written Southwell and his fellows out of the record, just as Donne did. As Raspa puts it, "there is deafeningly no mention of the executed Jesuit innocent, Robert Southwell" (xlv) in Donne's book. To that one can add that in Donne's benign version of the statist argument there is also no hint of the activities of Richard Topcliffe and his kind. Southwell's career as poet and as missioner exposes the abstraction and insubstantiality of the statist argument. In the Anglican system, Hooker's reasonableness, Herbert's piety, and Donne's own eloquence throve not only by the permission and patronage of the state, but under its frequently brutal protection as well. To Southwell's plea, "Overcome us by reason" (*Epistle,* 205a), like his predecessor Edmund Campion's request for "good method and plain dealing,"[9] the state had no answer but torture, trial, and death. Neither the poignancy of the plea nor the barbarity of the response is affected by the fact that Southwell and Campion, like Donne himself, accepted the principle that state and church are one under authority. The crucial question was, whose authority? Donne's acceptance of the authority of the state over religion preserved him for a long, spectacular career in the service of the state's religion; Southwell's rejection of it condemned him to death.

Even so, it would be easy enough to conclude that in this conflict of authorities we see a classic case of a transcendent ideology generating contradictions that destroy the people it has molded, all of whom are in some way parties to the violence and the horror of the results.[10] In the cases of Southwell and of Campion, however, there was a clear attempt to resolve just that contradiction by appeal to other principles, of reason and justice, and, in Southwell's case, compassion. Hence it is hard to see how Southwell is to be denied the status of martyr for what he called "soul rights" over the claims of the state. What brought him to the place of martyrdom and such an extreme assertion of the rights of the soul was hardly a devotion to the temporal power of the papacy; rather, as his youthful *Spiritual Exercises and Devotions* already reveals, it was his understanding of life lived as art, in his case the art of the imitation of Christ, expressed and discussed in his writing and consummated in his death. Thus, he became one of those whose life and work "calls into question All the Great Powers assume,"[11] and on that basis he has a profoundly important claim on our interest as poet and as man.

Yet it is in the nature of the question about Southwell's life and death that it cannot be left in a final resolution. Whatever else he was,

Southwell was a born poet who in normal circumstances might have produced a body of work comparable to any in his period. Like Shakespeare, he thought in metaphor, but unlike Shakespeare he seems to have believed in metaphor, sacrificing life and art to faith in the belief that things seen were the insubstantial signs of realities unseen. To many people of good will and intention besides Donne, it will have seemed an unnecessary sacrifice for an insubstantial end. Donne thought that the Jesuits' hunger for martyrdom was "inordinate" (*Pseudo-Martyr,* 119); moreover, given the nature of Southwell's conditioning and training, it must always be a question to what extent the sacrifice, when it came, was actually his own, and not that of his order or his church.

Donne objected strongly to the Jesuit vow of obedience because it "exceeded by its nature the moral scope of the life of the individual priest, [and] seemed to reach out . . . and encompass the entire contemporary political world" (*Pseudo-Martyr,* xlvi). It is also true that within the borders of the English national state, the claims of the state could be just as all-encompassing, and it is to Donne's credit that to the end of his life he remained uneasy with the statist argument and with his own advancement by it. Raspa believes that the missing two final chapters of *Pseudo-Martyr,* on the balance of secular and papal power in France, and on the conversion of Ethelbert of Kent by Roman missionaries, might "have ended up subverting the ostensible end of defending James I for which *Pseudo-Martyr* was written" (*Pseudo-Martyr,* liv). That is debatable. Donne's *Devotions* provide better evidence of his uneasiness. The fourteenth expostulation of the *Devotions,* read in the context of Donne's own background and subsequent history, will almost certainly remind Southwell's readers of his Saint Peter and the subject of his complaint: "This, *O my God,* my most blessed God, is a fearful *Crisis,* a fearful *Indication,* when we will study, and seek, and find, what days are fittest to forsake thee in; To say, Now, *Religion* is in a *Neutrality* in the *world,* and this is my *day,* the day of *liberty;* Now I may make *new friends* by changing my *old religion,* and this is my *day,* the *day of advancement.*"[12] At the crisis of his illness Donne evidently remembered the crisis of his life, in language, too, that refigures the question posed by Southwell's career: to whom, or to what, and on what terms, and with what possible mitigations, is loyalty owed? Robert Southwell's uncompromising answer shaped his life, defined his art, and killed him.

Notes and References

Preface

1. A. C. F. Beales, *Education under Penalty* (London: Athlone Press, 1963), 17; hereafter cited in text: "The increase of royal control under Edward VI after 1547, and under Elizabeth after 1558, was but a development within a theory of the supremacy already operative; and the reaction to Catholicism under Mary was not constitutional, but a change of direction only."

2. See Hugh Bowler, ed., *Recusant Roll No. 2 (1593–94),* Publications of the Catholic Record Society 57 (1965): viii.

3. On the question of the numbers of Protestants and Catholics under Elizabeth I, see Philip Hughes, *The Reformation in England,* 3 vols. (New York: Macmillan, 1954), 3:49, 122–28, 239; hereafter cited in text.

4. See *Mary Magdalen's Funeral Tears: A Facsimile Reproduction,* intro. Vincent B. Leitch (New York: Delmar, 1975), "The Epistle Dedicatorie" and "To the Reader." See also James H. McDonald and Nancy Pollard Brown, eds., *The Poems of Robert Southwell, S.J.* (Oxford: Clarendon Press, 1967), 1–2, 75; hereafter cited in text as *Poems.*

5. For a sample of his views on English character, see Robert Southwell, letter to Father-General Claudio Aquaviva, 31 August 1588, in John Hungerford Pollen, S.J., ed., *Unpublished Documents Relating to the English Martyrs, I,* Publications of the Catholic Record Society 5 (1908): 328; hereafter cited in text. On the potential success of the mission, see Southwell's companion and superior, Henry Garnet, letter to Aquaviva, July 1588, quoted by Christopher Devlin, *The Life of Robert Southwell, Poet and Martyr* (London: Longmans, Green, & Co., 1956), 161; hereafter cited in text: "The harvest . . . will be beyond measure."

6. Helen C. White, *Tudor Books of Saints and Martyrs* (Madison: University of Wisconsin Press, 1963), 257; hereafter cited in text.

7. For example, C. S. Lewis, *English Literature in the Sixteenth Century Excluding the Drama* (Oxford: Clarendon Press, 1954), 544–46; hereafter cited in text.

8. Pierre Janelle, *Robert Southwell the Writer: A Study in Religious Inspiration* (New York: Sheed & Ward, 1935); hereafter cited in text.

9. On Southwell's influence on Drayton, see Bernard H. Newdigate, *Michael Drayton and His Circle* (Oxford: Shakespeare Head Press, 1941), 215, and Christopher Devlin, "Southwell and Contemporary Writers, II," *The Month,* New Series 4, no. 3 (November 1950): 309–19. For recent comment on the existence of common ground between Catholic and Protestant, see Gary Taylor,

"Forms of Opposition: Shakespeare and Middleton," *English Literary Renaissance* 24 (1994): 283–314, and Marta Straznicky, "'Profane and Stoical Paradoxes': *The Tragedie of Mariam* and Sidneian Closet Drama," *English Literary Renaissance* 24 (1994): 112n2.

Chapter One

1. The Southwells were related to the Wriothesleys, earls of Southampton, and to the Cecils, Bacons, and Cokes (Devlin, 5, 15).

2. Nancy Pollard Brown, ed., *Two Letters and Short Rules of a Good Life* (Charlottesville: University Press of Virginia for The Folger Shakespeare Library, 1973), xxiii; hereafter cited in text as *Letters.*

3. Thomas Francis Knox, ed., *The First and Second Diaries of the English College, Douay,* 2 vols. (London: D. Nutt, 1878), 1:105; hereafter cited in text.

4. J.-M. de Buck, ed., and P. E. Hallett, trans., *Spiritual Exercises and Devotions of Blessed Robert Southwell, S.J.* (London: Sheed & Ward, 1931), 35; hereafter cited in text as *Exercises.*

5. Devlin, 29–30, names two confessors, both English: a Father Columb and a Jesuit, Thomas Darbishire.

6. Letter of 28 December 1588, quoted in Devlin, 181. Thomas Pounde of Belmont, Hampshire, presents an example of one of the first such young men. Captured and imprisoned in 1574, he requested admission to the Society of Jesus from prison and was accepted as a brother. See Hughes, 3:308–9, and Louise Imogen Guiney, ed., *Recusant Poets* (New York: Sheed & Ward, 1939), 182–86; hereafter cited in text.

7. Printed in Henry Foley, *Records of the English Province of the Society of Jesus,* 7 vols. (London: Burns and Oates, 1878), 4:288–330; see 292–99; hereafter cited in text. Southwell may have contributed to this *Life:* see Foley, 4:288, and Devlin, 340n18.

8. Stonyhurst MS. A.v.4, f.37, printed in John William Trotman, ed., *The Triumphs over Death* (London: Manresa Press, 1914), 69–70; hereafter cited in text as *Triumphs.*

9. John Gerard, *The Autobiography of an Elizabethan,* ed. and trans. Philip Caraman (London: Longmans, Green, & Co., 1951), 17; hereafter cited in text.

10. Pollen 1908, 317–18. In the next decade, the division between Jesuits and a significant party among the secular priests would reach England, breaking out first among imprisoned priests at Wisbech Castle, then reaching the public through the appellant or archpriest controversy of 1600–1601. See Peter Milward, *Religious Controversies of the Elizabethan Age* (Lincoln: University of Nebraska Press, 1977), 116–24.

11. Leo Hicks, S.J., ed., *Letters and Memorials of Father Robert Persons, S.J.: I (to 1588),* Publications of the Catholic Record Society 39 (1942): 227; hereafter cited in text. The date of Southwell's ordination is derived from a letter of

10 July 1584, in which Persons refers to Southwell as "Father" (Hicks, 215).

12. One of the recently discovered Roman letters shows him making the same request in an earlier letter of 23 January to Aquaviva. I owe this reference to Fr. Thomas M. McCoog.

13. Translation in Foley, 1:319. The original is printed in Henry More, *Historia Provinciae Anglicanae* (St. Omer, 1660), 182–83. The addressee is unknown. Devlin (99) thinks it was sent to John Deckers, but this is most unlikely. Pollen (1908, 307) suggests Aquaviva.

14. See Hughes, 3:335–96, "The Conflict," and especially 342–43, 362–63, 367–68.

15. She was the eldest daughter of Lord Dacres of the North. Her widowed mother married the third duke of Norfolk as his third wife, so that she became Philip Howard's stepsister. The duke contracted Philip and Anne in marriage when both were 12; the contract was ratified when they were 14 (*Triumphs,* 84).

16. Devlin, 131–33. See also John Hungerford Pollen, S.J., and William MacMahon, S.J., eds., *The Ven. Philip Howard, Earl of Arundel 1567–95: English Martyrs II,* Publications of the Catholic Record Society 21 (1919).

17. Nancy Pollard Brown, "Paperchase: The Dissemination of Catholic Texts in Elizabethan England," *English Manuscript Studies* 1 (1989): 120–43; hereafter cited in text.

18. John Morris, *Troubles of Our Catholic Forefathers,* 3 vols. (Farnborough, U.K.: Gregg International, 1970), 2:151.

19. Incomplete lists are provided by Pollen 1908, 293–333, and James H. McDonald, *The Poems and Prose Writings of Robert Southwell, S.J.: A Bibliographical Study* (Oxford: Printed for the Roxburghe Club, 1937), 63–65; hereafter cited in text. Devlin draws upon a group of letters that Philip Caraman, S.J., discovered in Rome in the Jesuit archives, but is inattentive to dates and references. Thomas M. McCoog, S.J., has prepared an edition of these letters, which was scheduled to appear in *Archivum Historicum Societatis Jesu* in 1995.

20. Pollen 1908, 329–30, with a partial translation in Foley, *Records* 1:324. The quotation is from Psalm 39.3.

21. Geoffrey Hill, "The Absolute Reasonableness of Robert Southwell," in *The Lords of Limit* (New York: Oxford University Press, 1984), 22; hereafter cited in text; Devlin, 210.

22. Augustus Jessopp, *One Generation of a Norfolk House,* 2d ed. (London: Burns & Oates, 1879), 70–71.

23. Topcliffe's bizarre spelling is modernized. The letter is frequently quoted by writers on Southwell, e.g., by Devlin, 283, who cites the original, BL MS. Lansdowne 72, f.113. "Trenchmore" was a fashionable dance. The first page of the letter is reproduced in Hughes 3: between 384–85, in company with two Privy Council warrants authorizing Topcliffe and Young to use torture.

24. Anthony G. Petti, ed., *The Letters and Dispatches of Richard Verstegan*

(c. 1550–1640), Publications of the Catholic Record Society 52 (1959); hereafter cited in text.

25. Devlin, 285. This account is drawn from material in Foley, 1:356–79; Pollen 1908, 333–37; and Devlin, 283–324.

26. In "Hope's Gambit: The Jesuitical, Protestant, Skeptical Origins of Donne's Heroic Ideal," *Studies in Philology* 91 (1994): 204, John Klause writes that Southwell "was not over-eager to throw his life away." This is true. The letter to Cecil is scrupulously written, yet there can be little doubt that the mercy asked for is the mercy of death rather than of release.

27. The first account, *A Brief Discourse of the Condemnation and Execution of Mr Robert Southwell,* is at Stonyhurst, MS. A.ii.1, printed by Foley, 3:164–75. Leake's account, also at Stonyhurst, MS. A.vi, is printed in Pollen 1908, 333–37.

28. Diego de Yepez, author of a very early Spanish history of the English persecution (1599), tells an attractive story of Southwell's being visited the night before his death by a nobleman, of the nobleman's subsequent conversation with the queen, and her regret for Southwell's death. Though quoted as true by Janelle, 85–86, and Devlin, 317–18, this uncorroborated story has the appearance of wishful fabrication.

29. A similar thin cord used to fasten Edmund Campion to his hurdle in 1581 is among the treasures of Stonyhurst College.

30. Verstegan, however, wrote to Persons, 30 March 1595: "He hanged until he was dead through the cry of the people, who would not suffer him sooner to be cut down, so great an impression his death did make within them" (Petti, 228).

Chapter Two

1. Anthony Raspa, *The Emotive Image: Jesuit Poetics in the English Renaissance* (Fort Worth: Texas Christian University Press, 1983), 11–34.

2. See A. O. Meyer, *England and the Catholic Church under Queen Elizabeth,* trans. J. R. McKee (London: K. Paul, Trench, Trubner, & Co., 1916), 190; see also Hill, 22.

3. To find this idea expressed with brutal literalness, see Henry Garnet's preface to Southwell's *Short Rule of Good Life:* "Yet is there a certain disposition in those which are chosen to so high a dignity [as martyrdom] ordinarily required of God, which is, first, to have killed their passions before they be killed by the persecutors . . . first to have become their own butchers before they be delivered to the hangman's shambles" (*Letters,* 90).

4. That there was competition between Jesuit and secular priests for influence in the Arundel family is revealed in *The Lives of Philip Howard . . . and of Anne Dacres His Wife,* ed. Henry Howard, 14th Duke of Norfolk (London: Hurst & Blackett, 1857), 221–22, composed by an anonymous Jesuit chaplain to the countess, who also writes that she was especially beneficial to the Jesuits and always had one in her house for more than 40 years.

5. Robert Southwell, *An Epistle of Comfort* (London: Secretly printed, 1587), 197a; hereafter cited in text as *Epistle.* A facsimile is available in *English Recusant Literature, 1538–1640*, sel. and ed. by D. M. Rogers (London: The Scolar Press, 1974), vol. 211.

6. See Hill, 29–30, for a good comment on the various glosses of this text.

7. John Bossy, *The English Catholic Community, 1570–1850* (New York: Oxford University Press, 1976), 24; hereafter cited in text.

8. The letter, which survives only in a retranslation of a Latin version, is printed in full by Foley, 3:335–36.

9. Quotations are from the first edition of 1591, modernized, and the work is hereafter cited in text as *Funeral Tears.* A facsimile edition is edited by Vincent B. Leitch (New York: Delmar, 1975).

10. Herbert J. Thurston, S.J., "Catholic Writers and Elizabethan Readers. II. Father Southwell the Euphuist," *The Month* 83 (1895): 233–34, 238; hereafter cited in text.

11. *Omelia Origenis de beata Maria Magdalena* (London, 1504?); *An Homilie of Marye Magdalen, declaring her fervent love and zeale toward Christ: written by that famous clerk Origene* (London, 1565); hereafter cited in text as *Homily.*

12. For example, compare, "If thou wilt that she faint not by the way refresh the bowels of her soul with the pleasants of thy taste" (*Homily,* sig. C4v) with, "If therefore thou wilt not have her to faint in the way, refresh her with that which her hunger requireth" (*Funeral Tears,* sig. H7v).

13. Mary's love for Jesus was, however, a traditional part of her legend. See Helen Meredith Garth, "Saint Mary Magdalene in Mediaeval Literature," *Johns Hopkins University Studies in Historical and Political Science* 67 (1949): 404–12.

14. Louis J. Puhl, S.J., *The Spiritual Exercises of St. Ignatius* (Chicago: Loyola University Press, 1951), 81–88. Puhl (170) demonstrates convincingly that the common translation of *composición viendo el lugar* as "composition of place" misrepresents the Spanish, and that the exact translation should be "a representation of the place by seeing it in the imagination." His own shortened version, substituting "mental" for "seeing in the imagination," while convenient, loses the important meaning, "seeing."

15. Brian Oxley, "'Simples Are By Compounds Farre Exceld': Southwell's Longer Latin Poems and 'St. Peters Complaint,'" *Recusant History* 17, no. 4 (October 1985): 332; hereafter cited in text.

16. "Epistle to the Reader."

17. Title from *Letters.* The title of the first published version was *An Epistle of a Religious Priest unto His Father.* This is preferable to the personal title adopted by Brown from Folger MS V.a.421. Since the text cited is hers, however, I have retained her title for consistency's sake, even though it seems that the first edition provides her copy text.

Chapter Three

1. *Triumphs,* xv. No sound edition of *Triumphs* is available. Trotman (cited previously, in chapter 1) took his text from BL Additional MS 10422, a text related to that underlying the quarto edition printed by John Busby in 1595, and paragraphed it ruthlessly. The quarto text is so bad that to cite it would be misleading and sometimes incomprehensible. Therefore, for convenience I have referred to Trotman's text, but quotations are from the Stonyhurst manuscript.

2. John Semple Smart, *Shakespeare, Truth and Tradition* (London: Edward Arnold, 1928), 64.

3. *Victoria County History of Warwickshire,* 3:60; *The Visitation of the County of Warwick in the Year 1619* (London: Publications of the Harleian Society, 1877), 12:93; *Pedigrees from the Visitation of Hampshire* (London: Publications of the Harleian Society, 1913), 64:223; hereafter cited in text as *Pedigrees.*

4. Mark Eccles, *Christopher Marlowe in London* (Cambridge: Cambridge University Press, 1934), 170; hereafter cited in text.

5. M. A. Shaaber, "The First Rape of Faire Hellen by John Trussell," *Shakespeare Quarterly* 8 (1957): 411–12; hereafter cited in text.

6. The fifth, in some ways most impressive, parallel is between Shakespeare's "I . . . vow to take advantage of all idle hours, till I have honored you with some graver labor" (*Venus and Adonis*) and Trussell's "Many months shall not pass, before I pleasure you with some more pleasing Poetry." Shaaber (415–16) says that this is a commonplace and quotes examples from Lodge, Spenser, Chettle, Barnes, Drayton, and others. On Shaaber's evidence, however, it looks as though Shakespeare took the idea from Spenser and Trussell took it from Shakespeare.

7. Trussell's text is related to the text of *Triumphs* contained in BL MS Additional 10422, and, according to Nancy Pollard Brown, the text of the poems in *Moeoniae* is similarly related to Additional 10422 (*Poems,* xlv). One concludes that Trussell's manuscript was an earlier exemplar of the same textual tradition.

8. "Late-sprung sectaries" are not necessarily only the extreme Protestants. In 1595 a Catholic writer could so describe all Protestants, including members of the Church of England.

9. The reference is to Psalm 83.4.

10. Janelle is quite wrong, however, to blame Southwell for chopping *Triumphs* into paragraphs, thus losing "one of the chief beauties of classical prose, the adaptation of its noble sweep to a long train of thought." The editor, Trotman, paragraphed the work.

11. The text quoted is Brown's, *Letters,* 23–73. The title is that of the first edition, printed by Henry Garnet from Southwell's own version. Brown's title, *Short Rules of a Good Life,* is from the Folger manuscript and has no authority.

12. The text in William Barrett's edition of 1620 (*STC* 22965) includes a dedicatory epistle to "M. D. S., Gentleman." It is a forgery. See *Letters,* liii, 98.

13. Robert Southwell, *An Humble Supplication to Her Majesty,* ed. R. C. Bald (Cambridge: University Press, 1953), 60–64; hereafter cited in text as *Supplication.*

14. The last Catholic petitioner, Southwell's kinsman Richard Shelley, had been imprisoned, and he died without trial (Devlin, 253).

15. The Babington Plot is still not completely understood. The plot attributed to Anthony Babington (a wealthy young Catholic gentleman) and his associates was the assassination of Elizabeth and the release of Mary Queen of Scots, timed to accompany a foreign invasion. The problem is that the term "Babington Plot" covers a wide range of actions and people, and no one knows just how deeply implicated in it the government itself was. Walshingham's spies were all over it. The standard accounts are by John Hungerford Pollen, *Mary Queen of Scots and the Babington Plot* (Edinburgh: Edinburgh University Press for Scottish Historical Society, 1922), and Conyers Read, *Sir Francis Walsingham,* 3 vols. (Oxford: Clarendon Press, 1925). Southwell, incidentally, was well-informed about the plot. A sentence in his first letter to Aquaviva after arriving in England, 25 July 1586, mentions "a matter in hand, which if it prove successful, bodes extremity of suffering to us; if unsuccessful, all will be right" (Pollen 1908, 308); Pollen believes this to be a reference to the plot before it was news. See John Hungerford Pollen, "Father Robert Southwell and the Babington Plot," *The Month* 119 (1911): 302–4, and Devlin, 248.

16. For this reading of the significance of King John, see F. W. Brownlow, *Two Shakespearean Sequences* (London: Macmillan Press, 1977), 78–94.

17. G. K. Chesterton, "The Secret People," in *Collected Poems* (London: Cecil Palmer, 1927), 157–60.

18. Southwell was reported as saying during a discussion of a possible Spanish invasion "that though the invaders might, yet would they not spare one Catholic in England, more than a Protestant (*Supplication,* xxi).

Chapter Four

1. Oscott College, Sutton Coldfield, Shelf RNN3.

2. Jean Robertson, "Robert Southwell's 'New Heaven, New Warre,'" *Huntington Library Quarterly* 45 (1982): 82–83, argues that "New Heaven, New Warre" is one poem, not two, and that the title is Southwell's own, anticipating Donne's and Herbert's way of "transferring some of the weight of the meaning of a poem from the text to its title."

3. Anthony Raspa, reviewing *The Poems of Robert Southwell,* disagreed with Brown's rejection of the Harmsworth manuscript's additional poems (*Renaissance Quarterly* 22 [1969]: 198–200).

4. Louis Martz, *Poetry of Meditation,* rev. ed. (New Haven: Yale

University Press, 1962), 182; hereafter cited in text; Hyder Edward Rollins, ed., *The Paradise of Dainty Devices (1576–1606)* (Cambridge: Harvard University Press, 1927), 132–33.

5. A. C. Partridge, ed. *The Tribe of Ben: Pre-Augustan Classical Verse in English* (1966; reprint, Columbia: University of South Carolina Press, 1970), 170.

6. Joseph D. Scallon, *The Poetry of Robert Southwell, S.J.* (Salzburg: Institut für Englische Sprache und Literatur, 1975), 74–75; hereafter cited in text.

7. For example, see Brown, *Poems,* xix–xxi and lxxix, who argues that the less original poems "may be literary exercises to regain facility in writing English. . . . It is to be expected that his first attempts at writing verse on his return to English would be mainly derivative, traditional in metrical forms, perhaps somewhat archaic in language."

8. Thomas Fuller, *The Worthies of England,* ed. John Freeman (London: Allen & Unwin, 1952), 536, tells of John Overall, Reguis Professor of Divinity at Cambridge, that when he became dean of St. Paul's and was required to preach to the queen, "he had spoken Latin so long, it was troublesome to him to speak English in a continued oration."

9. Wilfrid Kelly, ed., *The Liber Ruber of the English College Rome: I. Nomina Alumnorum 1579–1630,* Publications of the Catholic Record Society 34 (1940): 54.

10. Transcribed in Chirstobel M. Hood, *The Book of Robert Southwell* (Oxford: Basil Blackwell, 1926), 48; hereafter cited in text. I have modernized the spelling.

11. It is prefaced by an "Argument to the Reader" (sig. A4–A4v), undoubtedly written by the author, which misrepresents the poem, most likely for reasons of caution, as an allegory of fortune.

12. Herbert J. Thurston, S.J., "Father Southwell and His Peter's Plaint," *The Month* 106 (1905): 318–21.

13. Mario Praz, "Robert Southwell's 'Saint Peter's Complaint' and Its Italian Source," *Modern Language Review* 19 (1924): 273–90.

14. This is not actually correct. Towards the end of the poem Peter speaks of days and nights passing, of bad dreams, and even of finding himself in a graveyard, which, as Brian Oxley suggests, can only be the graveyard where Christ's body is lying: "Peter, unknown to himself, is keeping the first Holy Week vigil" (Oxley, 337).

15. Nancy Pollard Brown, "The Structure of Southwell's 'Saint Peter's Complaint,'" *Modern Language Review* 61 (1966): 5; hereafter cited in text.

16. Thomas Lodge, *Prosopopeia,* "Epistle to the Reader," attributes Peter's tears to his apostasy. See also L. J. Sundaram, "Robert Southwell's 'St. Peter's Complaint'—An Interpretation," in *Studies in Elizabethan Literature: Festschrift to Professor G. C. Bannerjee,* ed. P. S. Sastri (New Delhi: S. Chand, 1972), 4–9.

17. Helen C. White, "Southwell: Metaphysical and Baroque," *Modern Philology* 61 (1964): 165.

18. Isidore of Seville, *Liber Numerorum,* 12, "De undenario numero" (J. P. Migne, *Patrologiae cursus completus: series Latina* 83, col. 191). See also Russell A. Peck, "Number as Cosmic Language," in *Essays in the Numerical Criticism of Medieval Literature,* ed. Caroline D. Eckhardt (Lewisburg, Pa.: Bucknell University Press, 1980), 15–64.

19. As is the case with similar words in Southwell's poetry (e.g., "evil," "heaven"), the intervocalic *v* is lost in pronunciation.

20. *The Denial of Peter,* a picture by the Dutch baroque artist Hendrick Terbrugghen (1588–1629) in the Chicago Art Institute, offers a striking parallel to Southwell's conception. A brightly burning little fire slightly to the right of center foreground lights the figure of the maid, occupying the picture's right, as she rises to accuse Peter. Peter, sitting on the left, warmly dressed against the cold, less brightly lit by the fire, makes an extremely vulnerable figure as he recoils from the accusation. As Terbrugghen depicts it, the moment of denial is mental and precedes speech in a dark place dramatically lit by the fire, closely associated with the attractions as well as the authority of the woman, who is definitely depicted as malicious.

21. Devlin, 269–72. On the rape within a rape, see Sam Hynes, "The Rape of Tarquin," *Shakespeare Quarterly* 10 (1959): 451–53. John Crow, reviewing Devlin (*Shakespeare Quarterly* 9 [1958]: 73–76), owned to being put off, as an Anglican, by Devlin's Catholic view of Elizabethan history. Having disposed of Devlin's argument that the "W. S." of Southwell's dedicatory letter to his poems in the St. Omer edition of 1616 might be Shakespeare, Crow remarked in passing, "And I do not find myself persuaded by Fr. Devlin's later suggestion that Shakespeare's *Lucrece* must have been influenced by Southwell's work." Devlin's argument deserved better than that.

22. Hyder E. Rollins, ed., *Shakespeare: The Poems* (Philadelphia: Lippincott, 1938) 414: "A date for Lucrece of 1593–94 is firmly established."

23. The same paradox appears in Daniel's *Rosamond:* "Ah Beauty Syren, fair enchanting good, / Sweet silent rhetoric of persuading eyes: / Dumb eloquence, whose power doth move the blood."

24. This material previously appeared in Frank Brownlow, "Southwell and Shakespeare," *KM 80: A Birthday Album for Kenneth Muir* (Liverpool: Liverpool University Press, 1987), 27.

25. F. W. Brownlow, *Shakespeare, Harsnett, and the Devils of Denham* (Newark: University of Delaware Press, 1993), 129–31.

Chapter Five

1. Ben Jonson, *Works,* ed. C. H. Herford and Percy Simpson, 11 vols. (Oxford: Clarendon Press, 1925–52), 1:137.

2. Warren R. Maurer, "Spee, Southwell, and the Poetry of Meditation," *Comparative Literature* 15 (1963): 16; hereafter cited in text.

3. See, however, Harry Morris, "In Articulo Moris," *Tulane Studies in English* 11 (1961): 21–37, who acknowledges that the poems are imitations of love poetry but treats them (mistakenly) as autobiographical and written at the point of death, and singles out "I die alive" for close analysis.

4. Rosamund Tuve, "Sacred 'Parody' of Love Poetry, and Herbert," *Studies in the Renaissance* 8 (1961): 250; hereafter cited in text.

5. Brown did not print the Latin poems in her edition. They survive in manuscript at Stonyhurst and are available only in *The Complete Poems of Robert Southwell, S.J.,* ed. A. B. Grosart (Blackburn, 1872), 189–215. I owe my knowledge of these poems to two articles by Brian Oxley, "'Simples Are by Compounds Farre Exceld,'" cited previously, and "The Relation between Robert Southwell's Neo-Latin and English Poetry," *Recusant History* 17, no. 3 (May 1985): 201–7.

6. "Jonas" and the "ivy" are the Douay-Rheims, and Southwell's, equivalents of the more familiar King James version's "Jonah" and "gourd."

7. The near-complete subsumption of event into figure in this poem misled Carolyn A. Schten, "Southwell's 'Christ's Bloody Sweat': A Meditation on the Mass," *English Miscellany* 20 (1960): 75–80, into arguing that Nancy Brown was mistaken to link the poem with the other two Gethsemani poems. Schten mistook Southwell's treatment of Christ's sweat as a prefiguration of Calvary as a treatment of Calvary itself.

8. See Joseph G. Fucilla, "A Rhetorical Pattern in Renaissance and Baroque Poetry," *Studies in the Renaissance* 3 (1956): 23–48; cited by Brian Oxley, "The Relation between Robert Southwell's Neo-Latin and English Poetry," *Recusant History* 17, no. 3 (May 1985): 206. According to Fucilla, after being boycotted under Bembist influence in the midsixteenth century, this extremely mannered technique became popular again after about 1575.

9. The Harmsworth manuscript includes two extra stanzas that are probably discarded drafts. They do not belong in the finished poem as it appears in the other manuscripts.

10. G. K. Chesterton, *The Everlasting Man* (ca. 1925; reprint, New York: Dodd, Mead, 1946), 201–2.

11. τους κοσμοκρατορας του σκοτους τουτου, "cosmocrats of the dark aeon," in Christopher Dawson's translation, cited by John Lukacs, *Confessions of an Original Sinner* (New York: Ticknor and Fields, 1990), 306.

12. *The Oxford Book of Carols,* comp. Percy Dearmer, R. Vaughan Williams, and Martin Shaw (London: Oxford University Press, 1928), no. 170; hereafter cited in text as *Oxford Carols.*

13. Set by John Goss (1800–1880) and first published with the music in *Christmas Carols New and Old,* ed. Henry Ramsden Bramley and Sir John Stainer (London: Novello and Co., n.d.), 64–65. The text in *The New Oxford Book of Carols,* ed. Hugh Keyte and Andrew Parrot (Oxford: Oxford University Press, 1992), 340–41, is severely abridged.

14. Peter M. Daly, "Southwell's 'Burning Babe' and the Emblematic Practice," *Wascana Review* 3 (1968): 29–44.

15. Andrew Harnack, "Robert Southwell's 'The Burning Babe' and the Typology of Christmastide," *Kentucky Philological Association Bulletin* 4 (1977): 25–30.

16. J. R. Roberts, "The Influence of *The Spiritual Exercises* of St. Ignatius Loyola on the Nativity Poems of Robert Southwell," *Journal of English and Germanic Philology* 59 (1960): 455.

17. Herbert J. Thurston, "Some Physical Phenomena of Mysticism: Incendium Amoris," *The Month* 141 (1923): 535–47.

18. Hill (33) cites *Epistle of Comfort* as an example of Southwell's familiarity with the word: "If *Christ* was seen transfigured in *Mount Thabor* in glorious manner, he was also at the same time heard talking *de excessu* of his bitter passion" (32a).

19. As a friend pointed out to me, in an otherwise symbolic fire, the thorns have a very concrete look about them. One is tempted to associate them with the crown of thorns, but if the thorns too are symbolic, then they are probably the parabolic thorns of Matthew 13.22 and signify "the care of this world and the deceitfulness of riches." The same friend says that there may be a suggestion in "Justice" and "Mercy" of the Old and New Testament dispensations.

20. Helen C. White, "The Contemplative Element in Robert Southwell," *Catholic Historical Review* 48 (1962): 10.

21. *Byron's Letters and Journals,* ed. Leslie Marchand, 12 vols. (London: John Murray, 1973–82), 5:102: "Passed *whole woods of withered pines—all withered*—trunks stripped & barkless—branches lifeless—done by a single winter—their appearance reminded me of me & my family.—"

22. Three keyboard settings of Dowland's "lacrimae"—by Byrd, Farnaby, and Morley—appear in the recusant collection of virginal music, *The Fitzwilliam Virginal Book,* ed. J. A. Fuller Maitland and W. Barclay Squire, 2 vols. (New York: Dover Publications, 1963), 2:42, 172, 472.

23. Wilfird Mellers, *Harmonious Meeting* (London: Dennis Dobson, 1965), 43.

Chapter Six

1. For some of these works, see Herbert J. Thurston's "Father Southwell, the Popular Poet," *The Month* 83 (1895): 383–99, and Helen White's *Tudor Books of Saints and Martyrs,* 271–76.

2. On Drayton and Southwell, see Devlin, "Southwell and Contemporary Writers, II," 309–19.

3. John Bodenham, *Bodenham's Belvedere: or, The Garden of the Muses* (Manchester: For the Spenser Society, 1875).

4. Charles Crawford, "Belvedere, or the Garden of the Muses," *Englische Studien* 43 (1911): 204.

5. T. G. Holt, S.J., "Southey on Southwell," *Notes and Queries,* New Series 31 (March 1984): 54.

6. I am grateful to Thomas M. McCoog, S.J., who has very kindly let me consult his text of these Roman letters, to be published in *Archivum Historicum Societatis Iesu.*

7. John Donne, *Pseudo-Martyr,* ed. Anthony Raspa (Montreal: McGill-Queen's University Press, 1993), 150; hereafter cited in text.

8. For defending the immunities of the Church, Thomas was murdered in his own cathedral as he was about to say vespers.

9. Evelyn Waugh, *Edmund Campion* (Boston: Little, Brown, & Co., 1946), 237.

10. This seems to be the view of Ronald J. Corthell, "'The Secrecy of Man': Recusant Discourse and the Elizabethan Subject," *English Literary Renaissance* 19 (1989): 272–90. Corthell, incidentally, mistakes the anti-Jesuit spy in holy orders, Gilbert Gifford, for a Jesuit.

11. W. H. Auden, "In Praise of Limestone," *Nones* (New York: Random House, 1950), 15.

12. John Donne, *Devotions upon Emergent Occasions,* ed. Anthony Raspa (Montreal: McGill-Queen's University press, 1975), 74.

Selected Bibliography

The standard bibliography of Southwell's writings is James H. McDonald, *The Poems and Prose Writings of Robert Southwell, S.J.* (Oxford: Printed for the Roxburghe Club, 1937). It has been superseded, for the poetry, by Nancy Pollard Brown's work on the Clarendon Press edition of the poems.

Southwell's letters, written mostly in Latin, and surviving in a variety of sources and repositories, await a scholarly editor and translator. McDonald's list is now out of date, and published letters are scattered in various volumes in variously reliable texts and translations. About 40 years ago, Philip Caraman, S.J., found 12 letters in the Jesuit archives, Rome (*Fondo Gesuitico*, 651), to be published in *Archivum Historicum Societatis Iesu* (1995) in an edition by Thomas M. McCoog, S.J. Henry Foley, S.J., *Records of the English Province of the Society of Jesus.* 7 vols. (London: Burns and Oates, 1877), 1: 301–87 printed several of Southwell's letters and an eyewitness narrative of his trial and execution. Another group of letters is available in "The Letters of Father Robert Southwell" in John Hungerford Pollen, S.J. (editor), *Unpublished Documents Relating to the English Martyrs,* Publications of the Catholic Record Society 5 (1908): 293–333.

For a bibliographical guide to works on Southwell, see Vittorio F. Cavalli, "St. Robert Southwell, S.J.: A Selective Bibliographic Supplement to the Studies of Pierre Janelle and James H. McDonald," *Recusant History* 21 (1993): 297–304; see also John N. King, "Recent Studies in Southwell," *English Literary Renaissance* 13 (1983): 221–27.

PRIMARY SOURCES

An Epistle of Comfort. London: secretly printed, 1587. Facsimile reprint. In *English Recusant Literature, 1538–1640.* Selected and edited by D. M. Rogers. London: Scolar Press, 1974, vol. 211.

An Humble Supplication to Her Majestie. Edited by R. C. Bald. Cambridge: University Press, 1953.

Spiritual Exercises and Devotions. Edited by J.-M. De Buck and translated by P. E. Hallett. London: Sheed & Ward, 1931.

Mary Magdalen's Funeral Tears. London: Gabriel Cawood, 1591. Facsimile reprint. Edited by Vincent B. Leitch. New York: Delmar, 1975.

The Complete Poems of Robert Southwell. Edited by Alexander B. Grosart. London: Printed for Private Circulation [by Robson and Sons], 1872. Includes the Latin poems.

The Poems of Robert Southwell. Edited by James H. McDonald and Nancy Pollard Brown. Oxford: Clarendon Press, 1967. The standard edition. Excludes the Latin Poems. Inadequate commentary.

The Triumphs over Death. Edited by J. W. Trotman. London: Manresa Press, 1914. The only available text, fussily paragraphed, with an eccentric introduction.

Two Letters and Short Rules of a Good Life. Edited by Nancy Pollard Brown. Charlottesville: University Press of Virginia, for the Folger Shakespeare Library, 1973.

SECONDARY SOURCES

Beales, A. C. F. *Education under Penalty.* London: Athlone Press, 1963. A good account of English Catholic schools and colleges, including the English College, Rome.

Bossy, John. *The English Catholic Community, 1570–1850.* New York: Oxford University Press, 1976. An exceptionally good introduction to the world of the Catholic recusants and the missionary priests.

Brown, Nancy Pollard. "Paperchase: The Dissemination of Catholic Texts in Elizabethan England." *English Manuscript Studies* 1 (1989): 120–43. Excellent bibliographical detection, tracking the clandestine production of some Catholic texts in circles familiar to Southwell.

———. "The Structure of Southwell's 'Saint Peter's Complaint.'" *Modern Language Review* 61 (1966): 3–11. A useful but excessively didactic interpretation of the poem.

Cousins, A. D. *The Catholic Religious Poets from Southwell to Crashaw: A Critical History.* London: Sheed & Ward, 1991.

Devlin, Christopher. *The Life of Robert Southwell, Poet and Martyr.* London: Longmans, Green and Co., 1956. The only modern life of Southwell, well researched though sketchily documented, and well written, but from a strongly Catholic point of view.

———. "Southwell and Contemporary Writers. I." *The Month.* New Series 4, no. 3 (1950): 169–180.

———. "Southwell and Contemporary Writers. II." *The Month.* New Series 4, no. 5 (1950): 309–19. These articles give more detailed versions of material used in chapter 18 of Devlin's *Life.*

Hill, Geoffrey. "The Absolute Reasonableness of Robert Southwell." In *The Lords of Limit.* New York: Oxford University Press, 1984. A subtly argued analysis of the integrity of Southwell's prose by an important and sympathetic modern English poet.

Hughes, Philip. *The Reformation in England.* 3 vols. New York: Macmillan, 1954. The best modern Catholic history of the subject, indispensable to students of recusant writing.

Janelle, Pierre. *Robert Southwell the Writer: A Study in Religious Inspiration.* New York: Sheed & Ward, 1935. The first scholarly study, dated, but thoroughly researched and still useful.

Lewis, C. S. *English Literature in the Sixteenth Century Excluding the Drama.* Oxford: Clarendon Press, 1954. Contains a brief but generous notice of Southwell.

Martz, Louis. *The Poetry of Meditation.* Rev. ed. New Haven: Yale University. Press, 1962. Although not specifically about Southwell, this book argues that he is at the source of a tradition of Jesuit influence on English seventeenth-century lyric poetry.

Maurer, Warren R. "Spee, Southwell, and the Poetry of Meditation." *Comparative Literature* 15 (1963): 15–22. A refreshingly critical comparison of Southwell to a similar German Jesuit poet of the period.

Oxley, Brian. "The Relation between Robert Southwell's Neo-Latin and English Poetry." *Recusant History* 17, no. 3 (May 1985): 201–7.

———. "'Simples Are by Compounds Farre Exceld': Southwell's Longer Latin Poems and 'St Peters Complaint.'" *Recusant History* 17, no. 4 (October 1985): 330–40. These two short articles contain the most illuminating commentary and criticism on Southwell so far published.

Partridge, A. C., ed. *The Tribe of Ben: Pre-Augustan Classical Verse in English.* 1966. Reprint, Columbia: University of South Carolina Press, 1970. A brief but acute comment on Southwell's English.

Pollen, John Hungerford, S.J., and William MacMahon, S.J., eds. *The Ven. Philip Howard, Earl of Arundel 1567–95: English Martyrs II.* Catholic Record Society Publications 21 (1919). Gives a documented account of Southwell's relationship with Arundel.

Praz, Mario. "Robert Southwell's 'Saint Peter's Complaint' and Its Italian Source." *Modern Language Review* 19 (1924): 273–90. Places Southwell's long poem in its Counter-Reformation, Roman context.

Puhl, Louis J., S.J. *The Spiritual Exercises of St. Ignatius.* Chicago: Loyola University Press, 1951. An excellent scholarly translation for the student curious to know what the Exercises entail.

Raspa, Anthony. *The Emotive Image: Jesuit Poetics in the English Renaissance.* Fort Worth: Texas Christian University Press, 1983. The introductory chapter on the baroque worldview is particularly useful, though clumsily written.

Roberts, J. R. "The Influence of *The Spiritual Exercises* of St. Ignatius Loyola on the Nativity Poems of Robert Southwell." *Journal of English and Germanic Philology*

59 (1960): 450–56. Praises Southwell for the authenticity and simplicity of his religious feeling; an old-fashioned piece much influenced by Martz.

Robertson, Jean. "Robert Southwell's 'New heaven, new warre.'" *Huntington Library Quarterly* 45 (1982): 82–83. An important demurral about the Clarendon editors' handling of one of the most famous poems.

Scallon, Joseph D. *The Poetry of Robert Southwell, S.J.* Salzburg: Institut für Englische Sprache und Literatur, 1975. An excellent, well-informed, balanced book.

Sundaram, L. J. "Robert Southwell's 'St. Peter's Complaint'—An Interpretation." In *Studies in Elizabethan Literature: Festschrift to Professor G. C. Bannerjee.* Edited by P. S. Sastri. New Delhi: S. Chand, 1972, 4–9. Argues successfully that apostasy is an important theme of the poem.

Thurston, Herbert J. "Catholic Writers and Elizabethan Readers. II. Father Southwell the Euphuist." *The Month* 83 (1895): 231–45.

———. "Father Southwell, the Popular Poet." *The Month* 83 (1895): 383–99.

———. "Father Southwell and His Peter's Plaint." *The Month* 106 (1905): 318–21. These pioneering articles by an exceptionally learned Jesuit scholar are still worth reading for their historical interest and for the information they contain.

White, Helen C. *Tudor Books of Saints and Martyrs.* Madison: University of Wisconsin Press, 1963. Includes a general essay on Southwell relating his prose to the traditions of martyrological writing.

———. "Southwell: Metaphysical and Baroque." *Modern Philology* 61 (1964): 159–68.

———. "The Contemplative Element in Robert Southwell." *Catholic Historical Review* 48 (1962): 1–11. Helen White's interest in Southwell seems to have been chiefly religious, though her work is always learned and informative and has the great virtue of always taking him seriously.

Index

The Author

F. W. Brownlow was born in Northern Ireland and was educated at Wallasey Grammar School, the University of Liverpool, and the Shakespeare Institute (University of Birmingham). He has lived in North America since 1959. Currently Gwen and Allen Smith Professor in English at Mount Holyoke College, he has also taught at the University of Michigan, the University of Western Ontario, and Dartmouth College. His published work includes three other books, *Two Shakespearean Sequences*, *The Book of the Laurel*, and *Shakespeare, Harsnett, and the Devils of Denham*.